LOVED TO LIFE

BY JOHN MACDONALD

© Sonship Ministries 2019
www.sonship.co.uk

Loved to Life - by John MacDonald

Cover design & layout by Tom Carroll
Back cover photograph taken by Erin Dass

ISBN: 978-1-9165018-0-5

Loved to Life is available from Amazon: www.amazon.com in Paperback and Kindle format.

If you'd like to stay up to date with John MacDonald's latest publications, please visit his website:

www.sonship.co.uk

CONTENTS

ACKNOWLEDGEMENTS

So many people have influenced my life. If I haven't listed your name here, it isn't ingratitude. I am thankful to everyone who has walked with me and poured into my life, but there are a few individuals whose impact has had such far-reaching consequences for me.

First and foremost, my wife, Fiona who has seen me through the best and worst of times and whose love first taught me that I was loveable. I can never repay the debt.

My friends who have loved me despite me being... well, me: Alan and Catriona, Caroline, Sheila and Rab, Andy and Joanna, Niall and Pam, Steve and Cary.

A special thanks goes to James and Denise Jordan who shared and demonstrated life in this revelation of love in a way that connected with my heart. I am forever grateful to them for believing in me and being my friends.

The Fatherheart family for your encouragement, support and at times, straight talking. Many of you have walked with me through tears and joy, good and bad, and I am so grateful for your friendship and love: Mark H, Trevor and Linda, Mark G, Helene, Barry, Jeff, and La casa Galeano for providing the oasis where I was able to begin this project.

My mum and dad deserve much more than I could ever

give them. They gave me everything, then a little bit more.

And cheesy though it may be, I really am thankful to the Father who pursued me through everything until he could finally bring me home.

Mum in 1950s

Mum & Dad's Wedding Day 1960

Dad in the 1950s / 60s

PREFACE

This book is my attempt to explain how Divine love has changed my whole perspective of life. I don't intend it to be a biography, although I will share elements of my life journey. By dint of the fact that my journey is ongoing, it is obviously incomplete and merely a summary of where I have journeyed to thus far. By the time you read this, some of it may be out of date; so be it.

Whatever I have written in regard to other people's words or actions, please do not understand it as a criticism or judgement of those individuals. I am merely providing background to give the reader insight into the state of my own heart, which is in continual transformation and will continue to be so until I die or Jesus returns.

The views I express in writing are my own and should not be interpreted as a reflection of any ministry with which I have relationship nor of any individual other than me.

FOREWORD

Love is a word we are all familiar with. We use it regularly most days to describe our liking of, or affection for, someone or something to which we are drawn. In the past, I thought I knew about love; I have been with many women since my teenage years. I have "fallen in love" a few times, but I now know that I was completely ignorant of love's true depths and meaning.

The casual use of the word to indicate liking reflects society's casual attitude to what is, potentially, the most powerful force in the universe. We use it to describe an emotional response or desire for something that brings us personal gratification. That is often the focus, personal gratification.

I am discovering that real love is far from self-centred. Real love is always other centred; it always looks outward and never inward and is not interested in its own gratification. The power of true love is a force to be reckoned with.

Things such as strength, force, ruthlessness and toughness are seen as the necessary attributes for success in the world, the mark of winners. While the attributes of love, patience, kindness, selflessness, faith, and trust are seen as weaknesses to be exploited in others and eradicated in oneself.

Is it any wonder we have little regard for, or real understanding of, God who is described by the apostle John as love itself (1John 4)? Life taught me that it is to be grasped by the horns and wrestled into submission. Gentleness and kindness must be subdued in order to overcome; trust and selflessness cannot be embraced lest they create victims of us.

In recent years, many have begun to see beyond the casual understanding and selfish obsession with love into a vastness which not only fills the universe, but envelops all of creation, the planets and stars, even the void of space itself, in its embrace. Love is fearsome and awesome, yet it is nothing to fear. I am learning to embrace the reality of love that, at times, is painful yet exhilarating, mysterious and joyful and completely fulfilling.

This book is entirely subjective, written out of my own experience of love poured into my heart as an expression of my heavenly Father's affection for me.

I pray that your reading of this book will help you understand the depth of his affection for you and the lengths to which our Heavenly Father has gone to draw each of us to his own embrace.

Love & blessings,

— *John MacDonald*

EVERYTHING CHANGED

I will never forget that beautiful sunny August morning of 2005; it was the start of a whole new chapter of my life. We had recently returned from a month-long leaders' retreat in Toronto, and I was trying to prepare the next day's sermon. My wife, Fiona joined me for a short time. She played guitar, and we worshipped together until the Presence of God sat heavily upon us. As we sat in the stillness of His Presence, He spoke and my whole life changed from that moment on. It sounds dramatic, but it was the culmination of many years of God at work, mining my heart and preparing it for this moment.

During the time in Toronto, we spent a week under the ministry of James and Denise Jordan from New Zealand. I had heard James speak the previous year and enjoyed listening to him. What he spoke resonated in my heart, and I was looking forward to the week with him and listening to 'good teaching'. There were other speakers during that month, but James was the one I was eager to hear again.

I had no idea that the week would be one of the most significant times of my walk with God. As a believer for over twenty years, I had sought to be close to God, to be a man of God, to know Him and be used by Him. I had been to seminary and preached for most of those years. I was a pastor and had led many ministries and groups in church life, but James and Denise spoke of God in a way that I had rarely, if ever, heard before.

As the week began, they did not speak of a God who was like the God I learned about as a child, or like the master I was taught about in church. Nor did they present Him as the judge I heard of in Bible School. A deep longing for something more was awakened as I listened to the Jordans. Their words penetrated my heart and actually left me in much pain but also with a deep yearning to discover the God of whom they spoke.

Too often we are urged to ignore the voice of our heart and told to base everything on what has been written or spoken BUT our hearts are who we truly are. I could hear with my ears, understand and agree intellectually but too often my heart was uneasy at what I read or heard, but I was taught to subdue the instincts of my heart in favour of my intellect and the words of those wiser in the faith. I must admit that, often in my Christian experience, I was uncomfortable with what I was hearing from pulpits or reading in books, but I quelled my heart's unease and didn't realise I was extinguishing my ability to know the Lord as He truly is, because our walk with God is a heart issue not the acquisition of knowledge or development of intellect.

James and Denise spoke of God as a Father who loves me actively. They didn't speak about doctrine and theology (although they were biblical), they spoke of relationship but not relationship based on Bible reading, service, prayer and spiritual disciplines that I had preached and had heard preached. They spoke of a substance experienced, the very substance of God Himself who is love.

As I contemplated these things that August morning, I became aware of a deep and gentle presence enveloping me until I could only sit in silence, without thought, without utterance. Eventually, the presence spoke. As I sat in the armchair by my window, He spoke a single word to me. I knew the voice of Jesus. I heard Holy Spirit when He gave me prophesies and words of knowledge, but this was something else, deeper and more profound.

I heard the voice of the Father.

Don't ask me to explain how I knew it was Father, I knew in my spirit that this was the Father of Jesus speaking to me. His voice resonated within my heart, sounding so real, that even today I cannot tell if it was audible or internal; I only know it was real, far more real than the sound of my own voice. In a moment, I was brought to a place I had been trying to reach my entire life. All of my activity in church, my toughness in life had just been a little boy looking for assurance and validation. When He spoke that single word it started the process of putting to rest years of insecurity, fear and uncertainty about myself, my status as a man, and as a human being.

I had lived my whole life believing that being John MacDonald was not a good thing; that there was something wrong with me and I should be, indeed needed to be, someone else. For over forty years I thought being me was inadequate, being John was not enough to ensure my place in life and I spent so much energy and effort on being the John MacDonald I thought everyone wanted me to be. I was a social chameleon who could adapt to most situations but never felt as though I actually belonged in any of them.

I was conceived in 1960, outside of marriage, and just after I was born in April 1961, my dad was diagnosed with multiple sclerosis. This must have been a terrible shock for my mum, who was only twenty-two and my dad who was younger still at twenty-one. As I think back to what I was like in my early twenties and how I lived and looked at life, I have no idea how my parents coped with this incredibly difficult situation they were experiencing and the traumatic effect it must have had on them.

My mum wanted to have her children quickly rather than spaced years apart so within two months of my birth, my mum was expecting again. My sister was born the following March and my younger brother born the next year in August. In less than three years of their marriage, my mum and dad had three children while trying to come to terms with an increasingly debilitating disease affecting my dad, and all the uncertainty that comes with it. Additionally, my brother was born with some health issues that involved hospital visits and operations. This must have increased the stress and worry my parents were struggling to cope with. I remember the anxiety and tension it brought to me. Too young to comprehend it all, I had no real idea what was going on, but I do recall the fear I experienced.

Life was confusing from the beginning, fraught with worry, concern, and the sense that I was the cause of it all. It sounds irrational, but children are not rational thinkers, they are emotional creatures around which the whole world revolves and if something is wrong in that world then it must be their fault, something wrong with them. It is sad how many children consider themselves the cause of problems and disasters. Nothing made sense and circumstances as I grew up seemed to confirm that it was my fault and my parents resented my existence.

I remember as a two or three-year-old child, standing in our living room completely naked and just out of my dad's reach as he sat in his armchair. He was asking me to come closer so that he could put some clothes on me, but I was stubbornly and defiantly refusing his urging (by this time his walking was impaired, so he was unable to come to get me). In his frustration at my defiance and his own inability to come get me, he flicked his trouser belt at me. There was no real force in it and no malice, but his frustration at my insolence and disobedience, coupled with his inability to physically do anything about it, caused him to flick the belt at me. The buckle caught my thigh, and that did it. In my heart, it confirmed all of the false belief and blame: my dad resented me and blamed me for his predicament.

I remember saying, *"I'm telling my mum on you,"* as though that would scare him.

The belt did not mark me or injure me in any way; but from then on, I began to stop seeing my dad as a source of love and comfort. I didn't hate him or wish him harm, but I no longer thought of him as able to give me what I needed in terms of love, comfort, advice or affection. I felt rejected and abandoned and had it in my head that there was no one there for me. I now understand that it was then I began cutting my heart off from relationships and attachments that required dependency on another human being.

I got revenge for the incident. I threw dad's belt into our open coal fire when my dad wasn't looking. I have no memory of it, but my mum assures me I took great delight in doing it. It was an indication of how I would live my life going forward, reciprocating with acts of self-protection and defiance. As far as I was concerned growing up, it was me against the world.

As the years went on further incidents reinforced these wrong ideas and cemented my belief that I was an unwanted inconvenience. There were bouts of illness and infection (mumps, German Measles) that caused me to be separated from my siblings and quarantined. My sister and I were both in hospital at the same time for a tonsillectomy, although in different wards, so my mum would visit us both.

I was, perhaps nine years old, the only child in a ward full of adults. The whole experience was bewildering, embarrassing and frightening for me. One day the nurse asked me if my bowels had moved and I had no idea what she was talking about until an older man explained in more earthy language what she meant. I was so embarrassed at my ignorance and felt foolish. The evening after my operation, I remember the overwhelming feeling of aloneness and abandonment watching my mum leave the ward when visiting finished.

I was also sent to a residential home (as was my sister) so that the family could have respite. It was only for a couple of weeks, but it seemed to ram home the fact that I was the problem my family couldn't cope with. There, I was exposed to culture and behaviour I had never encountered and shouldn't have known about at that age. I was party to hearing and seeing things that such a young boy should not see, and it affected my understanding of sexual things in a way that was not healthy. No one touched me or did anything to me, but I was exposed to things I should not have been exposed to and it had an effect on me throughout my teen and even adult years. These older kids spoke in a way that was strange to me, of things I didn't have a clue about, and it reinforced the feeling of being an outsider, of not belonging.

During my primary school years, I was bullied by older boys in my neighbourhood, two in particular who left me feeling helpless, vulnerable and unprotected, which increased my frustration and internal rage. I don't know if these various incidents are behind my preference for my own company and a tendency toward introversion but that is how my life developed over the years. Even though I was amongst peers at school and on the streets, I didn't feel as though I fit; I didn't belong and had to create my own internal world in order to survive.

As a young child, I turned to reading. I read everything I could get my hands on simply because I could hide there. I could switch off and tune the world out. All the confusion, rejection, blame, and bullies faded into a background buzz and calmed my anxiety about life and the lack of surety and safety in the world around me. As I approached my teen years and beyond, alcohol and cigarettes became my hiding place (they made me look tougher than I really was) and later, fashion, music and sex and drugs became my refuge. I learned to keep people at a distance emotionally.

Violence was fairly common and all around me too; it was a normal part of life for most boys where I grew up, which was terrifying and traumatic. I was on constant alert to potential danger, violence and bullies. I couldn't be weak, otherwise I would become a victim. I had to toughen up and be part of the culture or be eaten up by it, feeling the pressure forcing me into 'proving' myself worthy of peer acceptance.

Because of my experiences of violence and gangs, I lived hyper-vigilant wherever I went. I was oversensitive to people around me and any threat they might pose. I was not really macho and tough, it was an act, an attempt at self-protection and fitting in. What I really wanted to do was hide from all the horror of life I was experiencing, with its constant fear and anxiety. Growing up, there was a terrific mix of fear and rage inside me that I didn't know how to cope with or find release from and I developed little 'coping' behaviours that I could retreat into to avoid facing the trauma that I was daily experiencing. These coping mechanisms eventually became patterns of life, some of which still live with me.

I had many questions about my life and the circumstances that shaped me and lived in a very 'orphan' fashion, without attachments and heart engagement. I could walk away from friendships and relationships with ease. Even as a believer, I saw myself as an outsider for most of my life – an inconvenience and the cause of my family's problems. I felt insignificant, inadequate and something less than I wanted to be, but Father saw, and still sees, something else.

Before the foundations of the earth were laid, He saw who I was to be. Father knew who John MacDonald should be and that is the lens through which He views me. My understanding of myself was completely opposite to how God saw me. Throughout the years of my life, He sought to draw me to the place where I would begin to realise who I really am as opposed to who I thought I was. He wanted to change my perspective of myself as well as my perspective of Him.

From a young age, on a number of occasions throughout many years, I remember hearing my name called in the street and turning around to look but finding the street empty. I saw things that no one else could see and it made me wonder if I was mad. It is only with hindsight, I realise God was reaching out to me, calling me to Himself but I did not understand that was what was happening.

On that August morning in 2005, my life had finally come to the point where I was able to hear what He wanted to say to me. After forty plus years, the day had arrived when God could speak to me what He always wanted me to hear. He had brought me to the place where He could lay bare His true feelings and opinion of me, and it came through that whisper in the humble surroundings of my spare room.

That moment which took so many years to arrive at has changed my life forever; I see myself, my experiences of life and my existence in an entirely different light. In that moment, God revealed Himself to me and I stopped asking the questions He never answers anyway. I saw God from a totally different perspective and now saw the questions as irrelevant. My understanding of everything is completely transformed by the inflow of love.

As I sat in the stillness of His presence and heard Him whisper to my heart, everything was changed in a moment, "in the twinkling of an eye" as Scripture would put it. One word changed the course of my life, ministry and my relationships as He told me who I have always been.

"Son."

That was it, three simple letters spoken with such tenderness and kindness that I had never experienced. I wept as that word, and all that it carried, touched the deepest parts of my being.

I sat in my chair and allowed His love to wash over me

as the tears flowed freely but it wasn't the wracking, painful sobs of a broken heart. Instead, I experienced the cleansing release of forty years of confusion and alienation. I had wept many times at altar calls and ministry sessions but never before had I experienced this release and sense of coming home that He gave me in that moment.

That one word held my identity, my calling, my security and affirmation. I sensed His pride in me and His pleasure in who I am. There was no trace of anything in His voice other than delight and love. I am someone's son and not just anyone's, Almighty God declared me to be His son and he my Father.

In that declaration was contained His promise to be the Father to me that I've never known, to do for me what my biological dad could not. He did not just speak to a forty-four-year-old man, He also spoke to that eleven-year old boy and comforted him too. Through no fault of his own, my dad, Angus could never give me what I needed growing up. He could not show me how to be a man, how to love or care and protect.

God himself was saying, *"I will do for you what your dad was not able to. I will ensure you know what it is to be loved and affirmed as a man, as a human being. I will father you now and do all of the things for you that your biological dad was unable to do."* All of this was contained in that simple utterance. I had no idea at the time how far reaching the effect of that word was going to be in my life. I still hear Him speak to me of my sonship, of His pleasure in me as His son and the joy my existence brings to His heart.

Is this how Jesus felt when He heard those words at His baptism (Matthew 3:17)? The affirmation of Jesus as a person, His identity confirmed as a son and feeling Father's joy in His existence must have been an overwhelming moment. When the unique Son of God needs to hear himself affirmed in this way, why would we think there is no need for us to know the same affirmation from the Father of our spirits.

I am convinced that every heart needs to hear the affirmation and loving approval of a father. It is not a once in a lifetime experience but an ongoing interactive communion. The actor Burt Reynolds (who passed away at the time of writing) seemed to understand this dilemma. In interviews, he was often asked what makes a man a man. Burt was wealthy, handsome and athletic. He was also a womaniser, drinker, and fighter. People saw him and others like him as the epitome of manhood and masculinity.

Growing up, Reynolds always idolized his father. His dad was a war hero who defended his country in WW2. It should come as no surprise that he wanted to be like his dad. Burt has regularly recalled that most of his childhood was spent trying to prove himself to his strict father. He wanted his father to be proud of him.

In his own words he tells us, *"My dad was the chief of police, and when he came into the room all the light and air went out. There's a saying in the south —no man is a man until his dad tells him he is. It means that someday when you're 30 or 40, grown up, this man whom you respect and love and you want to love, you hope he'll put his arms around you and tell you, "You're a man now, and you don't have to do all those crazy things you're doing and get into fistfights and all that to defend your honour. You don't have to prove anything to me. You're a man and I love you."*

But my dad and me, we never hugged and never kissed, and we never said, "I love you." No, we never even cried together. So, what happened was later, I was desperately looking for someone who would say, "Burt you're all grown up now, and I approve of you, I love you, you don't have to do those things anymore." But that didn't happen, and I was lost inside.

For most of my life, I couldn't connect—I was incomplete; and I didn't know then what I needed to know." [1]

Even a star like Burt Reynolds felt the need for a father or father figure to tell him who he is but he never received that affirmation. All of his 'masculine' behaviour was a child

---

1.   Parade Magazine

trying to get his daddy's approval, to live up to his exacting standards but the little boy within Burt never could.

Countless numbers of boys and men are in the same predicament. No one has told us how important we are; no one has ever said that they are proud of us. It seemed as though nothing was ever good enough, none of our attempts at pleasing or impressing ever seemed to have the desired effect of a man saying to us, *"I love you, son. I'm proud of the man you are."* I was completely overwhelmed when I heard and felt that approval and affirmation. Needless to say, my sermon for the next morning changed.

The rest of that day was a kind of blur, I don't recall what I did or how I spent the rest of it, but I do remember being afraid to go to sleep that evening in case the feeling evaporated while I slept. I need not have feared. *"he who began a good work in you will carry it on to completion until the day of Christ Jesus."* (Philippians 1:6).

I continue to grow in the realisation and truth of who he made me to be. It is a lifelong journey and the process will only be complete when Jesus returns, but on that August day, I discovered the wonderful truth of who I am, and I am now enjoying the journey of life.

I have begun to like being who John MacDonald is: *"Son."*

It is no longer theology; it became and is still, a relational and experiential reality. His love is being poured into my being daily and is causing transformation that none of my previous 'Christian' behaviour, activity and discipline ever could. I tried as best as I knew how, to become the kind of man of God I thought he wanted me to be. All of my attempts, disciplines of prayer and fasting couldn't accomplish anything near what that one word has accomplished in my life.

The simple word spoken, '*Son*', that continues to be spoken is defining how I live my life. It frees me from the treadmill of religious activity as a means of validating my existence or placating God's considerable (and imagined) annoyance with my sinfulness. I have adjusted to who John is supposed to be and have begun to embrace the real me, allowing love to shape who I am becoming. All of my attempts at holiness, godliness and spirituality seem laughable now as I am continually realising the power of His love to accomplish within me all that the things of man and religion were previously unable to achieve.

I am learning to allow love to show me what sonship looks like and I am having the time of my life!

Dad with Grandpa MacDonald & Uncle Robert.

CHAPTER 2

THE WORLD TURNS BLACK

Another major event that took place in my life occurred on a Friday afternoon in September 1972, when my dad's aunt Peggy and uncle Robert met us at the school gates. We saw more of Peggy and Robert than we did of my paternal grandmother, but this was unusual. They had never come to meet us at school before, and it struck me as odd at the time. My memories are dimmed by the passing of time, but I recall walking in the local park with Peggy and Robert and my brother and sister, enjoying the sunshine and the pleasant surprise of eating ice cream with no urgency to get home.

Eventually, we did set off for home, and I noticed as we approached the house that the curtains were closed. I was aware enough at eleven years old to know that closed curtains[2] on a sunny afternoon were not a good sign. My mum was waiting for us in the bedroom I shared with

---

2. *When I was growing up curtains were closed when a death had occurred in the home.*

my brother, sitting on the edge of the bed. As we came in and stood before her, I recall her saying, *"Your dad isn't coming home."*

By that point, he was in a hospital in Glasgow where he often went for family respite, but I knew immediately what she meant. I knew what not coming back meant. The news was so sudden and unexpected. My dad would never return home and I didn't get to say goodbye.

That same day, we were sent to my newly married cousin's home on the other side of the city for a few days. It was not until we were there that I realised we would not be allowed to attend the funeral the following week. I was livid and contacted the parish priest behind my mum's back and asked to be one of the altar boys serving at the funeral mass. But my mum had *"gone behind my back"* first and told the priest that if I made such a request, his answer should be a firm no. This only served to increase my anger and frustration and for over thirty years, I held it against my mum that she never allowed me to say a proper goodbye. She did it with the best intentions; I understand that now, but a child doesn't reason like that.

The feeling was that funerals were not places for children to be so you can only imagine how incensed I was to discover my younger cousin was taken to my dad's funeral by my aunt. It was a wound that would mark me for many years.

Around the time of my birth, my dad started displaying strange behaviour, so his workmates contacted my grandfather to say that they had noticed something wasn't right about my dad at work. This led to a series of doctor and hospital appointments and just after I was born, he was diagnosed with multiple sclerosis, which turned out to be progressive and quite aggressive. My dad's ability to speak was severely affected so it was difficult and frustrating for him to communicate his needs and feelings. He lost his sight, only seeing shadows. He lost his motor functions so that eventually I and my siblings would be the ones to brush his teeth for him, give him drinks from a specially adapted cup with a spout and spoon feed him his meals and light his cigarettes.

I cannot remember my dad walking unaided. I remember him with a walking stick (which was still around the house into my teens), then a walking frame followed by a wheelchair until he became bedbound.

My dad's long-term illness was traumatic, but his death was unimaginably painful, and I didn't know how to process the grief, the anger and loss. It was not only the grief and pain of his death, but the years of being deprived of his fathering and guidance and love. There was no real consciousness of what I had lost, though there was a profound sense that everything had changed, and I had no way of expressing what I was feeling at the time. But my heart knew it.

I did have an overwhelming sense of pain, helplessness and anger I couldn't express or form words to describe. After his death, I would wake up in the middle of the night, literally in a sweat, knowing I wasn't good enough to go to heaven and if I lived for a million years, I could never be good enough to get there. I was terrified of that idea. I would lie in bed silently asking my dad to speak to God and do something on my behalf. I figured my dad, having suffered as he did, might have more influence in heaven and cut down my time in purgatory.

I thought a lot about death and dying, it constantly occupied my thoughts. I would dream of my own funeral and wonder who would come to it. My waking hours were also filled with such imagery. This went on well into adulthood and even now occasionally haunts my dreams.

During my stay with my cousin, her life obviously continued. I remember one evening I stayed with her brother-in-law and to my shame, I wet the bed for the first time in many, many years. To my gratitude, no one brought it up. In fact, the brother-in-law gave me a gift of a Rod Stewart record called *You wear it Well*. Even today, listening to that takes me right back in my memories and the song, as much as I love it, is inextricably linked to the loss of my dad.

That weekend my cousin's friend visited, her toddler was playing with his cars and continually crashing them into the fireside hearth. I found this insufferable and exploded before running into the bedroom. I threw myself on the bed and I remember, while I was lying there, face down crying, I vowed that, "*I'll never let them see me cry.*" I cried a lot over my dad's absence in private but never in front of people. I wasn't going to be that weak.

For years, the slightest little noises enraged me, and it is only as Father has been loving me that I realised the little boy who lost his dad and erupted that day in 1972, was always there, reacting in so many ways throughout the changing circumstances of my life. In many of the events I experienced throughout my youth and adult years, emotionally I was being thrown back to 1972, and all the feelings of resentment, frustration and helpless anger would burst out and flood over those around me.

I never saw my mum grieve over my dad (though she most certainly did in private). Unconsciously, I learned that I needed to be strong and resilient, to be able to cope and be capable, an attitude that continued well into adulthood despite the reality being different.

So many go on with the struggle of being strong, saying and doing the right things, looking capable and competent until it all comes crashing down on them. The adversarial nature of our society prevents them from revealing the true depths of despair and unhappiness that lurks within. That was me; I would never admit need and was always 'capable'. Until the times when I was not capable displayed in small bouts of illness, which were psychosomatic ways of escaping pressures and circumstances I could not cope with.

There were obvious difficulties and pains that accompanied my dad's illness. Once he was diagnosed, then his working life was over and his career as an electrician ended. We were living, basically, in poverty. There were times when Mum had to choose between eating for herself and feeding her children (she always chose us).

If my dad had lived, we would, in all likelihood, have been in a different lifestyle. Being an electrician in the ship-building industry did not satisfy him. In his ambition to achieve more and provide for his family, he attended night school. On reflection, I could see him, had he lived, perhaps establishing his own business and providing apprenticeships for my brother and myself. What a different life we would have had. Instead, we relied on my maternal grandmother's generosity and things like 'Provident' loans[3] and handouts from the local St. Vincent de Paul (a Catholic Church organisation) to meet many of our basic needs.

There was not the same kind of developed social security system as we have in the United Kingdom today. When I began school in 1966, my mum was given a child-sized

---

3. Provident was a loans company which provided vouchers to be spent in certain stores.

'*Donkey Jacket*' [4] instead of a school blazer. I wasn't aware of the shame over this, but I picked it up from the adults around me, along with the anger at such injustice. An over-heightened sense of anger and injustice stayed with me for most of my life.

I remember when I was around ten or eleven years old and beginning to get interested in girls, we didn't have any money to buy me a school uniform and I was sent to school in a pair of wellington boots under my mum's old ski pants (the kind with elastic straps under the feet, no fly opening and no pockets). It's difficult to impress a girl while wearing wellington boots and your mum's trousers. In fact, it's just about impossible.

Most of the clothes I had were bought with the assistance of my maternal grandmother. She would take us to the Stirling Stephen store in Glasgow's Virginia Street, where she had an account, and would never buy me the kind of clothes my peers wore. Instead of Levis or Wrangler jeans, she would buy Brutus brushed denim and instead of Adidas shoes I would get Clark's Commandos. Some of my clothes were provided as hand me downs from older cousins whose style choices were not the same as mine so I would refuse to wear them, never aware of how difficult it was for my mum to make ends meet. Today, I realise that my penchant for

---

4.   A Donkey jacket is a traditional workman's jacket, typically worn by road sweepers and other manual workers

nice clothes is rooted in the disappointment and shame of those years (additionally, I look good in them).

As I mentioned earlier, I had the idea that it was all my fault – the illness, poverty and death was a result of my being born and being present in this world. As a result, some of my difficult behaviour was a reaction to those internal feelings that I could not articulate. I began displaying all the typical signs of a child traumatised by bereavement, many of which have stayed with me throughout my life. I am convinced we have underestimated the extent of the trauma inflicted upon our young people, at an early age, by seemingly everyday, innocuous circumstances.

According to research carried out by the U.K. based 'Childhood Research Centre',[5] _bereavement is different for children under twelve years old._ When compared to older children, bereavement for under twelves is more likely to result in them developing psychiatric difficulties. These can manifest in a number of ways, including anxiety, depressive symptoms, fears, angry outbursts and educational underachievement along with lower self-esteem, and it seems that male children react more severely than female children.

Disobedience, violence and criminal activity, drug taking, and alcohol abuse are all possible consequences of repressed bereavement grief. I easily hit every one of those markers

---

5.   The report can be downloaded from www.cwrc.ac.uk/news/1233.html

and still see some of it manifesting in my life today. This is common for people who have not processed childhood loss. They are not necessarily bad people, just damaged.

When my father died, I felt bereft, abandoned, totally alone and powerless. The support networks for children and families we see in place today did not exist in the early 1970s, so not only did I feel alone, I really was left alone by the adult world to cope with the emotional devastation and trauma of losing my dad. I have only begun to understand the crippling effect it has had on my life. Back then, the medical and teaching professions were not fully conversant with the effect of parental loss on children and were in the dark regarding treatment. I'm not sure they even believed that children could be affected by it much.

Being told by many adults that I was now the *"man of the family,"* made me feel as though I had to grow up and be responsible. I took their admonitions seriously and believed that it was my duty to look after the family. People mean well when they say these things, but it puts incredible pressure on children to adopt adult behaviour they are not emotionally, intellectually or physically mature enough to bear. My inability to live up to this standard increased the levels of anxiety I was experiencing and led to elevated levels of behavioural problems, especially conflict with my mother and siblings. I felt as though I was failing in my duty to my mother and siblings.

In addition to those things, trying to be the man of the family created an unconscious but over heightened sense of responsibility in me to support and help vulnerable girls and women. I missed so many romantic opportunities in my younger years because I wanted to rescue and befriend rather than kiss the girls. That was a great hindrance in my romantic aspirations. Each girl or woman I befriended or helped, was a representation of my mum, and it was her I was trying to rescue.

I only realised this recently when I had an unfortunate, and angry, encounter with someone I overheard speaking ill of my mum. My reaction was way over the top, beyond what could reasonably be expected in the circumstances. It was embarrassing and irrational. As I prayed and examined the incident, Holy Spirit showed me I was still eleven years old, trying to be the man of the family, the protector and rescuer.

We say that children are resilient, and they will 'get over it,' I don't know if we really believe that to be true, or if it is the excuse we use because we don't know how to handle the trauma and grief, ourselves. How can we comfort and heal the damage done when we ourselves have never known the comfort and healing that love can bring to our own pain. So many of us are living with unresolved trauma and pretending that "it didn't do me any harm". Yet, often the harm is obvious for all to see.

I had been relatively innocent up until the time of my dad's passing, reading superhero comics, playing child games and lots of sport. I ran 4x100 relay at school, played soccer and rugby, but after his death, I started to take more risks, hanging out with older boys, discovering alcohol and cigarettes, engaging in gang activity and getting into fights more frequently. Fighting and acting tough became a way of life, of fitting in to the teen culture around me; even our games contained elements of risk where injuries were common.

I felt for much of my life, that my life was not in my own hands and in fact was in the control of others, which created a real sense of injustice and resentment in me. The death of my father and my helpless inability to do anything about it, the feeling of being powerless and impotent as I faced bullies alone, and no one listening to me or paying attention to my needs, increased that sense of injustice and resentment. Much of my anger and behavioural issues stemmed from this.

The technical term is *"external locus of control,"* and I believe is what we see manifesting when we read of road rage and violence that seems to make no sense whatsoever in today's society. These are people reacting to a little boy or little girl's sense of having no control over, or say in, their own lives and life circumstances, reacting out of helplessness and powerlessness. That is not to excuse such behaviour, but it does help to understand it.

My seething anger and explosions of rage were a result of feeling that others were responsible for the difficulties and trials of my life. It caused me to isolate myself emotionally and avoid attachment or deep connection to others. I began to have regular bouts of illness that I now realise were psychosomatic in nature as a result of my psychological distress. Again, there is a technical term for this: "*somatisation.*" For me, it was minor illnesses that enabled me to withdraw from the world; colds, sniffles etc. allowing me to avoid people and social situations – even into adulthood. Anxiety and depression became a huge part of my life, along with violent behaviour, stealing and dodging school.

I never spoke to anyone about what was happening or what I was feeling, and sadly, not one adult asked me about it or seemed to pay any attention to what might be happening in my world. As I reacted, the adults around me only became stricter and more insistent on punishment and discipline. Being called to the headmaster's room or other teachers to receive corporal punishment became a normal part of my school day.

No teachers, priests or family members seemed to take much interest or offer anything in the way of support. Back then, the thinking was that if you were punished at school it must have been deserved (to be honest it usually was) but no one understood why. In fact, my wider family were conspicuous by their lack of involvement and almost total absence from my life. At the time I most needed guidance, I felt there was not one person who was making any attempt to provide it other than the guys from the street gangs, whom I could never openly speak to about my struggles.

During those growing years, it was as though no one understood what it was like to be me and in the face of it all, I decided that I was alone in the world; I could and would only ever rely on myself.

I stopped being a child at that time.

I would look at adults and feel frustrated by how they treated me; I couldn't wait to grow up and be free from their control and interference. This attitude remained with me throughout my life and was the cause of a number of lost life opportunities.

THE WAY IT WAS

We moved home from Glasgow, a city of around 800,000 people, to a much smaller town called Cumbernauld, in 1975, and it took some time before I could find a school to attend. I had to compromise on the subjects I was able to study, so my attitude was not at its best. I hadn't had a say in the house move (I still thought of myself as the man). When I eventually started classes in the school I had not wanted to attend to begin with, I encountered hostility from the first teacher whose class I sat in.

1973/ 1974 School Photograph

In a simple exchange lasting no more than a few seconds, a boy asked me if I had an eraser, to which I replied I did not. Immediately the teacher began shouting and bawling at me, saying that she would not tolerate troublemakers in her classes and telling me to get out of her classroom. That made my mind up in regard to my new school. I had been dubious about going there to begin with, now there was no doubt; they could all take a running jump as far as I was concerned.

I hardened so much that I became a problem for every teacher I had at that school until I left prematurely in 1977. I would disregard teacher commands; if I wanted to leave the class, I did when I felt like it. I would refuse the corporal punishment that was administered in those days. In Scotland teachers would use a thick strip of leather called a 'tawse' to hit children on the palm of the hand with. Of course, in some teachers' enthusiasm the result was not only a red palm but bruised wrists. Supposedly only a maximum of six strikes could be given but some teachers found a way round this by giving six on each hand.

I would deliberately dress in disregard for the uniform rules. I fought and gambled on school premises and dodged school as often as possible. I was such a different child from the boy who contested the Dux award at primary school only a few years previously. It got so bad that each absence from school would be followed up by a phone call from school to my mother at her workplace, checking whether the absence was authorised (of course they never were). Despite all that must have been in my written records, not one of them noticed how I had suddenly changed or thought to connect my behaviour and attitude with the death of my dad; so I was written off as a troublemaker. Of course, I responded to that by being one.

Even beyond school years, I was a difficult person with an attitude. I became increasingly aggressive and involved in violence. I had to pass through hostile gang territory on the way to and from school, and I never went without a weapon in my school bag. Thankfully, I never had to draw that weapon on my school journeys. I became hyper-vigilant and aware of my surroundings, sensitive to the possibilities of violence and danger.

Unconsciously, people became sources of danger or of 'getting' something from, and the older I got, the more selfish I became and the more I saw others as people to take from. I had learned to protect myself and wasn't going to make myself vulnerable ever again. By using people, I distanced myself emotionally from them. As I look back, I can see that most of my life decisions, experiences and relationships were directed by this traumatic part of my life. I made inner vows and resolutions, which further isolated me and closed down my ability to open up to people, to love and receive comfort.

It was so bad that when I was first married and my wife would put her arms around me in bed at night, I would often tense up and ask her not to touch me. I didn't know what to do with love, how to let it in or how to respond to it. Love and comfort were alien, so I isolated myself emotionally. I had grown up without overt demonstrations or displays of affection and when it was offered as an adult, I didn't know what to do with it. Even though inwardly, I was craving it. Deep down, I believed the best way to avoid pain was to cut off any hope of ever having something permanent in my life. I could walk away from jobs, friendships, romances, almost everything without regret.

I gave up on my academic ambitions and left school with only minor qualifications. It left me with a huge sense of inadequacy and failure, along with the feeling that the world owed me something. At age sixteen, I gave up on my career ambitions when I was denied an apprenticeship at a large engineering firm. My uncle had a barber shop and spoke for me to one of his customers who was a director at the firm. I sailed through the written tests and to the final interview but was unsuccessful. Weeks later the director asked my uncle how I was getting on in my new apprenticeship. He was surprised when my uncle told him I had been unsuccessful but promised to enquire more. Later he said to my uncle, "I'm sorry, you didn't tell me what school he went to." In West of Scotland code that meant, "You didn't tell me he was Roman Catholic." This fuelled my anger at what I perceived to be injustice, directed personally at me, throughout my life and actually increased any prejudice I felt toward Protestants.

I left home at seventeen years old and only came back to the family home as a stopgap while I obtained a flat or a job elsewhere. I spent so much time drifting from job to job, romance to romance and friendship group to friendship group. Even as a Christian, I still had those walls around my heart. That little boy held his fortress well. It was truly secure, locked up tight and impenetrable. I talked a good game about God's love and mercy, but it didn't penetrate to any real depth. As I look around, I see so many people, believers included, who have never been able to process the traumas of childhood. We pretend to have everything together, to be big and strong, and capable but all the while inside there is a little boy, a little girl who needs to be loved.

As I get older, the biggest regret I have is the way I disconnected from my mum and my siblings. Even today, we don't have the closeness that I would wish for. The tragic, early death of my dad damaged each one of us, and I was too wrapped up in myself for so many years to the extent that I acted as though I didn't have a family. That is probably my greatest sadness. It's not that we don't speak, of course we do. But through the years, I have, for the most part, kept out of their lives and the lives of my nieces and nephews.

In the world we live in we face difficulties, disasters and disappointments. The natural proclivity is to deflect and blame as Adam did in the Garden of Eden (Genesis 3:12). I blamed the whole world for my problems, but the truth is there is no one at fault. What happened to me was not the result of some awful conspiracy to ruin my life, it happens to thousands of children around the globe, and over the generations our children have grown up to be the broken adults that I became. We see the results all around us in broken cultures and societies everywhere.

Thank God in this revelation of Father, I have discovered love that comforts and heals. He has been with me throughout it all. I can look back and see moments in my life where He pursued and stuck by me, carrying me through many difficult times until eventually, His love became the healing balm and comfort for my deepest wounds. The reality of being loved by Him is causing transformation to take place from within rather than by external influences.

As I am learning to be loved, I am finding the comfort that was missing, throughout my childhood and youth is being applied to my soul. I am discovering that my past does not need to dictate my present.

Love really is making a difference!

His love poured into my life has been, and continues to be, a reassuring and comforting balm to my whole being. Love given without conditions and no demand for performance or achievement on my part has given me a real sense of who I am, what my worth is. Love is lifting from my shoulders the weight of blame and shame I carried

for so many years. There is no magic wand for the things
that trouble us. Religion wants something instant, but the
'instant' fix is not a lasting thing. It fades into oblivion, and
we become addicted to chasing another 'fix'.

Love is in no hurry (1 Corinthians 13:4); it only has
our best interests in mind. As we own our brokenness and
weakness love is more able to exert its powerful influence
upon our souls' brokenness and wounds. That is what I am
experiencing and, as a result of Father being a Father to me,
my soul is becoming like a little child weaned at its mother's
breast (Psalms 131:2).

CHAPTER 4

GOD IS GOOD?

In the midst of all my confusion growing up I always had a sense of there being a God, whatever I conceived Him to be. At one point in my childhood, I thought He might be an alien spaceman from another planet. This conclusion was arrived at thanks to a man called Erich von Däniken who wrote a book and made a documentary film of it,[6] which I went to the cinema to see around 1970/71. It made sense to me at the time, although now I think it is one of the nuttiest things I've ever heard.

Throughout my childhood, strange things would happen in my life that I couldn't explain. I would see and hear things no one else heard or saw. I remember staying at my aunt's house and seeing faces at the window of a bedroom one floor up. When I told my aunt, she scolded me for frightening my younger brother and cousin, so I learned to keep quiet about the things I 'saw'. These things freaked me out a lot

---

6.   Chariots of the Gods? Published by Putnam 1968, The movie being released in 1970

and confirmed all my misconceptions about myself, but I never spoke to anyone about them. I kept them to myself, wore my masks and continued to keep people at a distance so they would never discover how weird I really was.

Shortly after my dad's death, I stopped attending church. Instead of going to Catholic Mass, I would spend time with friends each Sunday. It was a long time before I told my mum though. This was the first sign of how I had been affected by my dad's death. Until then, I had been quite serious about my religion, even thinking of the priesthood and quite earnest in my desire to please God and help the priests. Around the time of the Biafran crisis of the late 1960s, I remember telling people I wanted to go to Africa to tell them about Jesus (even though I didn't actually know Jesus or much about Him).

When I was ten or eleven years old, we had a School visit from a priest belonging to the Marist Brothers (*a Catholic Brotherhood dedicated "to make Jesus Christ known and loved through the education of young people, especially those most neglected"*) and I looked into studying for the priesthood. It was progressing quite well, and I was looking forward to attending their school and then seminary. But it mysteriously came to an end one evening while I was playing soccer for my school. They were to visit me at home, but no one showed up, and I heard no more from them. I was absolutely desolate and felt, yet again, that there was something wrong with me that I would receive such rejection. On reflection, I am fairly certain it was the intervention of my mother, horrified at the thought of her little boy living in one of those places.

If God was there, He seemed far away from my experience and certainly not interested in my small insignificant life. If only I had known. I never realised, until many years later, that my weird experiences as a child were that same God reaching out to me and it was His calling I was sensing. I never heard anyone in church speak of that kind of stuff, not at the Catholic Church nor at the Baptist Kid's Club. The nuns and priests in school didn't mention it at all, so I kept it quiet so that I wouldn't be locked up in a mental ward.

One of the saddest things is the number of kids I've spoken to who have had similar experiences and haven't told anyone because they thought they would be sent to the psychiatrist's office to deal with their mental episodes. They have unnecessarily suffered in silence, thinking that they were losing their minds. We need to stop telling our kids silly bible stories and getting them to draw burning bushes and swords. Their Father is supernatural, and they experience His supernatural ways as they journey through life. If we don't explain it to them, we condemn them to a life of shame, fear and eventually, abandonment of faith.

When my dad died, God seemed further away than ever,

and I eventually stopped trying to pray to him, stopped going to mass and confession, gave up being an Altar Boy and thought religion was a waste of time. By the time I was twelve years old, I had stopped going to church completely. I began to lose interest in the boys' clubs I belonged to, including the cub scouts. In light of all that had and was happening, they seemed irrelevant to me. When it came to God, I was confused, uncertain and always questioning.

My mother came from a family with strong Protestant roots, belonging to the Orange Order and the Freemasons, although my mother herself did not get involved in it. My father came from a family whose roots were firmly in Roman Catholicism. My maternal Grandmother was very active in the local church and seemed to spend more time there than anywhere else. Neither side of the family was nominal in their commitment, they were all deeply entrenched in their respective groups and beliefs. On meeting my father and deciding to get married, my mother converted to Roman Catholicism and agreed to bring the children up in the Roman Catholic Church (although I never knew my mum to ever attend RC mass). I guess it was quite contentious for my relatives on both sides of that union. I remember an uncle phoning my sister when she was a young teenager telling her to never marry a Roman Catholic. His sister (my mum) and both of his female cousins had done just that, and it was obviously something that ate at him over time. I believe it was probably the main reason why we saw little of my mum and dad's families and remain estranged today.

I grew up going to Sunday mass and also served as an altar boy for a number of years at many RC ceremonies, including a few of my relatives' weddings, but I never really understood any of it. The mystery of God remained just that, a mystery. The priests seemed fierce and terrifying. I remember one priest who would order parents with crying children out of the church during services and another who would hear confession with the dividing privacy curtain left open so that he could better identify who was speaking. Another priest had to be moved to another parish as his drinking could no longer be hidden or kept quiet.

In addition, there seemed to be no place for children in the Roman Catholic Church community I belonged to (and which my parents never attended). I was forced to go to masses that passed right over my head and attend church related groups which did not really explain anything. Every month, the scout troupe I went to was required to attend Sunday mass together and I recall one occasion where one of the boys didn't attend. At Scouts meeting the following midweek, he admitted attending a Baptist church instead for a family event. The scout leader smacked him on the face and shouted at him, so I decided to keep quiet about my doubts. Though I would still sneak off to the Baptist church midweek kid's club where they talked about Jesus and God loving us.

They told us God was nice, which I was never sure about. To me, God was angry, demanding and capricious and some of the priests, nuns and teachers, and now scout leaders, I knew reinforced that idea. If God really was good and nice, then why did He punish my family for my existence? What was so wrong with me being alive that God made my dad and my brother sick and my family poor? If He was so amazing why not heal my dad?

My dad died at age thirty-two when I was eleven years old. Where was God then? If He loved me, why didn't He stop that from happening and allow me to grow up with a dad who would teach me about manhood? I was definitely not convinced of God's goodness and niceness; in fact, I thought He wasn't even listening to or watching what was going on in my life. I kept hearing my paternal grandmother, who was a devout churchgoer, bemoaning the misfortune of my dad's illness as the cross that she had to bear (even though she had nothing to do with my dad's care). It increased my resentment toward God because it seemed as though God had chosen to inflict this upon our family.

I came to the conclusion that my conception and birth was the catalyst for all of these problems; that this indicated God's displeasure and He was punishing us for my existence. With all of the confusion, poverty, etc. as my background, it was no wonder I could never see God as anything other than distant and uninterested. The best I could hope for from

Him was a few thousand years in purgatory if I managed to be 'good'. I had tried being good and where did that get me? Orphaned (in my thinking) was where it left me, with no one to look out for me except myself. I was truly convinced there was no one on my side, no one who would look out for me or have my back.

I became 'a tough guy' outwardly, because of my fear and confusion. That was the pattern for the rest of my life – even as a believer. I covered up the brokenness with an outward show and attitude that belied the inner turmoil, fear and shame. I am convinced this is the reason the world sees churchgoers as hypocrites. They see our brokenness and shame and they see the false covering, our fig leaves of self-righteousness, false piety and judgmental attitudes and do not want to be part of that system.

Large parts of my childhood seemed normal, but I always felt like an outsider. I recall a Pastor telling me that when he saw me, he saw someone who thought he was always on the outside looking in, his nose pressed up against the window wishing he was a part of what was going on but had been excluded. It was as though there was something the world wasn't telling me; I wasn't privy to the secret and I did feel excluded. Of course, there was no secret, it was my perception of myself and everything around me, which gave the impression I didn't belong. It seemed to be magnified with the death of my dad and no one seemed to show any interest in me, or how it affected me.

I began to 'act out' as people call it. School became drudgery and I started skipping classes. By the time I was fourteen years old, I was regularly missing weeks and months at a time, hanging out in houses with other school-dodging friends, finding plenty of mischief to keep us occupied. When the new school session began after summer break in August of 1975, I decided not to go back. I didn't return to school until December of that year after we relocated to another town. Even then, my times of dodging lessons continued much as it had in my previous city. My life pretty much continued this way into my twenties as violence, alcohol, sex, drugs and rock 'n' roll replaced books and comics. Unbeknown to me, I was piling up trauma after trauma.

God was most definitely out of the picture as far as I was concerned. My life became much more exciting in some ways, but also more tense and traumatic due to the ongoing violence, uncertainty, and the unpredictability of my surroundings and those people I mingled with. Many of the boys I hung out with and encountered in fights had been exposed to as much if not worse trauma than me and some seemed to have no conscience or morals. We deemed them the 'mental' ones; boys who were so crazy, violent and unrestrained that there was nothing they wouldn't do

1970s Glasgow was a violent place and most weekends would erupt with violence in the dance halls and streets of the city. My group of friends were no different, and we regularly became involved in 'action'. Even if we weren't looking for it and didn't want it, it seemed to find us. Knife crime was rampant, and it is only grace that kept me from more police arrests and being more seriously hurt than I was.

Greece 1984

CHAPTER 5

GOD IS REAL!

The apostle Paul speaks of God as "*the Father of compassion and the God of all comfort, who comforts us in all our troubles...*" That had never been my experience of God – He was too distant and disinterested and when it came to people, I have no memory of being comforted, no modeling of pain management, no examples of how to process my traumatic experiences and frustration, except in anger - that was mostly what was modeled to me at home, in school and on the streets. Why would God be any different? He was a source of fear and intimidation to me. Anger was the only emotion I had no problem expressing.

I never received nor sought comfort in my painful experiences of childhood or youth except in the many vices I was discovering. As far as I was concerned, there was no comfort available to me and I bottled up the pain and 'toughed' it out or drank it into silence or temporarily soothed myself with sex. I didn't speak of the effect upon me or how these experiences made me feel. As a child, I never told my mum lest she tried grounding me or overprotected me, and I never spoke of it with friends, afraid they would think I was weak - not "one of the boys". I realise now, at an older and (hopefully) wiser age that most of my friends were feeling the same.

Looking back, I can see that throughout my childhood and into adulthood, I would experience periods of what I now recognise as depression, accompanied by anxiety manifested in a sense of continually being ill at ease. In addition, I would often become sick with niggling little colds, bugs and pains. Subconsciously I had found a way to avoid the sense of being overwhelmed by life and its decisions; I could hide from problems and dodge social situations, avoid confronting issues by being sick. None of this was conscious or deliberate, it was the cumulative effect of years of pressure, anxiety and trauma bearing down and causing my system to react by closing off. I had found a way to protect myself.

If I were not closing down, then I would regularly mouth off and explode with anger and rage, often accompanied by violence. There is a long list of fights at school, at home, in the streets; holes kicked or punched in doors and walls, job losses through my attitude and self-destructive behaviours in my past which, at the time, I was at a loss to explain. My usual explanation was to find fault with what others had done or said to cause my irrational outbursts. I now understand it was the result of trauma and unresolved emotional wounds, the most devastating of which was my dad's untimely death. That is no excuse for the things I did and said but it has helped me to understand myself a little better.

In March of 1985, a few weeks short of my twenty-fourth birthday, I was introduced to the young girl who would eventually become my long-suffering wife. She was on a night out with her work colleagues who also happened to

be acquaintances of mine. I discovered later that her friends had realised how naïve she was and warned her to watch herself with "*that guy*." I must have impressed her as she agreed

Wedding Day 1985

to a date the following evening and then kept me waiting as she was thirty minutes late. Fiona and I married the following September.

As we continued to date, I began staying over at her parents' home, sleeping in her older brother's bedroom. I was into the party lifestyle. I was running club nights and promoting live music in a Glasgow nightclub each Thursday evening or out clubbing and partying most nights, so my cycle was to sleep in the day and live at night. On the evenings I stayed over at Fiona's parents' home, I would stay up late at night reading. I read every book in her brother's collection until all that was left were his Christian books.

During this period, I had begun to bump into old friends who were now '*into Jesus.*' I thought they had done too many drugs, too much acid. I would try and avoid them but somehow kept bumping into them in places I wouldn't have expected to meet them. I couldn't be bothered listening to the religious nonsense they spouted at me and would try to hide in the pub, but they found me in the pub. It was all really weird, so I avoided the Jesus stuff as much as possible and that included those books of my girlfriend's brother.

Eventually, I did pick up a couple of the books that were written about guys with tougher backgrounds than mine. In reality, my life was not as tough or traumatic as many of my contemporaries who experienced greater levels of violence in the home, as well as outside, but my own experience of life was painful and confusing in its own way, leaving me frustrated, afraid and bewildered.

One of the books I read was Nicky Cruz's story *Run, Baby, Run*, which reminded me of the lifestyle of some of my younger years. The other book was by an ex Hell's Angel named Brian Greenaway. In younger years, I used to read pulp novels about Hell's Angels and skinheads, so his book intrigued me. As I read his story, I cried (in private,

obviously). I began to realise that Jesus was actually who/
what I needed, but I had no idea how to get there and grew
frustrated. I was not going to ask anyone about it because
that would blow my image. I recalled conversations with
my paternal grandmother when she would try to convince
me to return to the Roman Catholic Church and I'd tell
her, "I'll get around to God someday." That was how I had
left things regarding God; I'd get around to him some day.
After meeting Fiona, I had no idea that day was looming.

One Sunday in November 1985, Fiona's brother invited
me to accompany the family to a church service he would be
preaching at in their Presbyterian church. I had been getting
more attached to Fiona and, by extension, her family so I
agreed to go along. There was no special emotion or great
sense of expectation attached to my acceptance, I thought
I'd go along to please the family. I can't remember how I
was feeling that day nor much about the church service.
I remember bowing my head during a time of prayer and
thinking, "*Well, here I am. I've done sex, drugs, rock 'n' roll
and even politics. I guess you're what's left to try, so let's give it
a go.*" Hardly the classic 'sinner's prayer'! But as I left that
church, I couldn't stop smiling and feeling happier than I
had in a long time. One thing disturbed me. What was I
going to tell Fiona?

I had the strangest idea in my head that I could not
shift. The recurring thought was, "*I need to stop sleeping*

with Fiona." That was the craziest idea I'd ever had, and I've had a few, but it persisted all throughout the drive back to Fiona's parents' house for dinner. Once there, I took the opportunity to speak to Fiona in the kitchen, alone. I have no idea which of us spoke first, but we both had the same thing to say. *"We need to stop sleeping together."* There it was. Perhaps this God thing is real after all, I mean who could have predicted that only twenty-four hours previously?

If someone had told me of these events in advance, I would have scoffed at them and thought them to be mad; stop sleeping with my girlfriend? Give up sex because I went to church? But there you have it. I went to church and stopped having sex with my girlfriend and that was the first of many changes.

It turned out that God gave Fiona a choice between him and me as we sat in separate sections of the church that day. Fiona chose him and got me in the bargain. At the time it was joyous, but salvation didn't erase my past or mend my brokenness. I'm sure over the years she must have questioned that 'bargain'. Our relationship was subject to my moods, anger, control and selfishness. My pain and brokenness were not only affecting me, I inflicted them upon my beautiful wife who had not known such things in her life before.

HIDING BEHIND FIG LEAVES

Many people say that once you're saved, everything is gone, sin, pain and grief is all dealt with by the cross and taken away by Jesus, we are new creations and the past is gone. But that is a denial of reality. We still struggle emotionally. We still have anger outbursts, feelings of inadequacy and doubt. Christian believers still lean toward self-reliance and human efforts at godliness and righteousness. We even carry a tendency toward sin in our efforts at self-comfort.

The truth is that due to Adam's failure in the Garden of Eden, our humanity is fractured at the very core. This fracture will exist until Jesus returns and no amount of denial, or ministry, will change that truth. Of course, as we encounter love, there will be increasing measures of healing, but we will still be broken human beings in a fallen environment that challenges our humanity. That is the legacy of the man and woman after Eden. The sooner we can come to terms with our own brokenness, the easier it will be to live at peace with ourselves, be more tolerant and less judgmental of ourselves and other people's brokenness and imperfection, and the easier it will be to enter into the rest and contentment of His loving embrace.

Brokenness was never his plan for us; being loved was always Father's intent for his children but the brokenness, caused by the relationship breakdown in the Garden of Eden, became the very thing that blocked us from receiving His love. He never stopped loving us, humanity stopped receiving His love and we chose our own fig leaves over His comfort and love.

When man 'sinned', he changed how he related to God. He didn't approach his Father in the same way, he hid and cringed in fear. His perspective of who God is changed, and God was no longer viewed as the loving Father who created the wonderful environment, they lived in. Instead, He became someone to be feared and appeased.

I wonder where the man and his wife got the idea that God would punish them. Was there a seed of doubt planted by the serpent, perhaps? What was it about their eyes being opened that introduced the fear of punishment into their experience? Whatever it was, it resigned mankind to a life of continual judgement. Not from God but from ourselves. We now judge what is right or wrong, good or bad, holy and unholy, and we have set ourselves up as the regulators of morality. Man judged God and decided that God was unhappy with him and something needed to be done to make God happy again. Our judging has led to a whole code of behaviour intended to turn 'Angry God' back into 'Happy God,' but only if we keep to the code.

God the Father never withdrew His love; man withdrew his fellowship and covered himself with something other than love. The man's attempts at covering up and making himself acceptable became the foundation of religion and our codes of conduct. All of our religious practices and traditions, all of our systems and programmes are merely sophisticated fig leaves aimed at diverting an angry deity's retribution. All of our religious activity is an attempt to hide behind something so that our nakedness and brokenness can't be seen. The reality is that, just as the man and woman couldn't truly hide their nakedness, neither can we. There is nothing adequate to the task except His love.

That's what my life had been founded on; fig leaves that made me feel invulnerable and safe. I learned to have an act, to keep it all together, play cool and not let any cracks appear, but all that pain and trauma was still there, simmering under the surface. My carefully crafted image was just that, an image, an illusion and fig leaf that protected me from being 'found out' and exposed as a fraud. All my energy went into protecting that projection by any means:

lies, trickery, pretenses and emotional distancing among them. I worked hard at being John MacDonald. But, as it turns out, I was trying to be someone else and wouldn't allow John MacDonald to be truly seen by anyone. I even fooled myself. I wore the right clothes, listened to the right music, fought when I needed to fight and strutted when I needed to strut. I was cool, unaffected (so I thought) and able to keep people at a distance so they would never see the scared little boy hiding in this big suit of armour who desperately needed to be loved but didn't know how to accept it.

As a believer, I carried on the same way - keeping my act together, being a good religious performer who served at every opportunity, witnessed, attended the meetings and followed the code; I even led early morning prayer meetings at 6am. My life was not so different from before, I was still pretending, only now, Jesus was a big part of my life and I loved him. The difference now was that my fig leaves were new, shiny, religious ones to give the impression of holiness, godliness and humility.

The right spirituality makes one popular, so I pursued that, fitting in by memorising scriptures (much to my wife's chagrin and my pride), serving enthusiastically, attending all the meetings, tithing and giving and learning the jargon. I thought I was genuinely pursuing Jesus and godliness, but I was still living the life of that little boy who wanted his dad to say, *"I love you. I'm proud of you,"* the little boy who was afraid for people to see the real, broken John.

As I became aware of being broken, the spiritual journey became a quest to get fixed and sorted so that I could be 'normal'. The sense of being something other than I should be is something we all struggle with. A whole industry has arisen, secular and sacred, which attempts to capitalise on this sense of not being 'right'. Everyone wants to be someone else, to be normal and acceptable or even to be a star and have our fifteen minutes of fame. Believers are not immune to this as we chase titles, positions and status in ministry. The world is reflected in our ambitions, competition and selfish egotism.

In secular society, the need to be fixed is linked to success and achievement, wealth and power. People are encouraged to get fixed in order to be 'normal'. Normal becomes the standard everyone is striving for. In Christian culture, our broken humanity can be seen as an offence to God, an obstacle to living as He demands, and it needs to be sorted out, to get fixed; thus, the need for so many ministries and therapies. Unless we are 'fixed' God cannot use us in ministry. Using the same language as the secular self-help material, the language of success and achievement, wealth and power, we strive to reach this esoteric standard of 'normal' Christian living.

Inner healing, emotional healing, whatever term you prefer, I pursued it. I went to counselling, prayer ministry, healing courses galore. Some of it was helpful in some areas, but I wasn't fixed. I wasn't normal. I had gotten it into my head that I need to be fixed so that I could serve God, so that I could be used of God in building His kingdom. My brokenness was an offence to the great God of heaven and earth, my creator. In this world, broken things are either fixed or discarded and I did not want to be discarded. I thought if I was broken, I was useless to God. But as love has been poured into my heart, as it has been soaking into my being, I have discovered great truth that I want to share with those of us who think we are disposable and valueless to God.

Firstly, God has no desire to 'use' us. He does not need you or me to achieve his purposes. He is God and can do as He pleases without any human help, yet He deigns to invite us to join him in his realm of activity. We are given the great privilege of joining Him in His endeavours. How could we be so arrogant as to think God 'needs' us to accomplish His purposes on earth? He is not in need of servants; He has a whole host of them dedicated to doing His will on earth and heaven. These servants have been following His commands perfectly for millennia even before there was a human being on planet earth.

To which of the angels did God ever say, "Sit at my right

hand until I make your enemies a footstool for your feet"? Are not all angels ministering spirits sent to serve those who will inherit salvation? Hebrews 1:13-14

In contrasting the angels with Jesus, the son, the writer reminds us of the angels' status as servants of God whom He commands on behalf of those inheriting salvation (Psalm 91:9-11). Contrary to popular thinking we do not command angels. I have heard so much of people having conversations with angels as though the angels were their servants. I don't think these are the angels of the Bible they are speaking with. The angels of Scripture are commanded by God alone not human beings.

Those in Christ are like Mephibosheth who thought of himself as nothing, disqualified by his disability, yet sat with his brokenness hidden beneath the king's table. The king's servants gave him the same service they offered to the king (2Samuel 9:1-13). Mephibosheth sat in a place of great honour where he had previously expected harsh treatment and rejection. The wonderful thing is that he could not walk to the table by himself; the servants had to carry him there. His brokenness was not an obstruction to favour. In fact, it was his 'entry fee' to a position of honour. In the same way, we do not seek entry to Father's love and embrace by our activities, spirituality or performance. Our brokenness is not a barrier to experiencing the favour of God.

Jesus has opened the way to Father's bosom (John 14:6) and Father himself gives the revelation and impartation of love as he did in the Garden of Eden (Genesis 2:7). Father gently calls us to his own bosom rather than harshly commanding or rejecting us. The angels of heaven serve our needs at that place. His great love covers our broken humanity (Proverbs 10:12; 1Peter 4:8) and as that love replaced the man's fig leaves in the Garden (Genesis 3:21) and King David's table hid Mephibosheth's withered legs so the Father's Love spreads over His children that they might not be crushed by the awful realisation of how far from perfection they are. God is not seeking servants, but sons and daughters who know the covering of His great love for them and are invited into His most intimate place of abiding, where servants visit but do not dwell.

Secondly, we do not build the kingdom and have never been instructed to do so. We are told to seek the kingdom (Matthew 6:33; Luke 12:31). In other words, to dwell in the place of relationship and inheritance gifted to us by our Father. Rather than encouraging us to build something by our efforts, Jesus tells us in Luke 12:32, *"Do not be afraid, little flock, for your Father has been pleased to give you the kingdom.* The writer of Hebrews in 12:28 says, "*...we are receiving a kingdom that cannot be shaken."* The kingdom is not something we build; it is something we receive as a gift from our Papa, out of His sheer delight in you and me as His children. The kingdom already exists, that's why we pray that God would manifest his kingdom here on earth (Matthew 6:10).

The apostle Paul prayed that the eyes of our hearts would be opened to see the kingdom (Ephesians 1:18). Jesus told the Pharisees, "...*The kingdom of God does not come with your careful observation, nor will people say, 'Here it is,' or 'There it is,' because the kingdom of God is within you*" (Luke 17:20-21).

All of our attempts at kingdom building and encouraging the faithful to get out and build the kingdom are really worldly shows of ostentation and selfish ambition. Like the Pharisees, we are driven by the need to prove our worth through performance and achievement and what these urgings actually do is feed the selfish ambition and pride, that our brokenness gives birth to. The apostles Paul and James have things to say about selfish ambition in ministry and none of it is good (Philippians 1:17; 2:3; James 3:14-16).

We fill peoples' heads with stories about being history makers and world changers and we send them out with bold words ringing in their ears, burning them out in time to be replaced by the next batch of zealous and ambitious individuals. I was totally caught up in that ostentation and selfish ambition for ministry, and I pursued 'getting fixed' to help make it possible. I knew early in my Christian life that I was called by God to preach and I thought it was up to me to 'get ready' and pursue that calling.

I have since learned that the calling of God can take many years before it matures in an individual, and it is He who does the readying of His ministers. Look at King David's life and the many years God took in preparing him. Between his anointing and kingship were many years of struggle as the Lord shaped a king out of a shepherd boy. I believe that we are too often putting people into ministry positions before they are mature enough or ready for it. We reason that God has given us a 'mission' therefore we need to gather an army to make it happen. The problem is that we end up with a high attrition rate as many realise the futility of their attempts at winning the world for Jesus, and we see multitudes of wounded saints, which we blame the devil, the world or their own inadequacies for.

I had great visions of myself as an anointed man of God and spent many years trying to make it happen. Inwardly I railed against those I thought were obstructing me but in reality, I was a little boy who did not know much of God's reality and that was obvious to many. The calling, equipping and commissioning of men and women of God is a work of the Spirit in a person's heart and no amount of study, desire, activity, eagerness or gifting will speed up that process in our lives. No amount of ministry will fix you enough to equip you for such calling as God gives to His ministers.

No amount of healing prayer can put in you what God wishes you to have in order to fulfill the call. No amount of ministry is going to give you the character of heart that is necessary in the work of the Kingdom and no amount of training will give you the gift you lack. These are all works of Holy Spirit over many years. I'm not saying healing prayer or training isn't helpful. It can be and has been for me, but it cannot make you something you are not. And it cannot give you anything God has not given you either. But how I tried; for over nineteen years, I worked to make myself fit for the calling. I went to bible school, attended courses, volunteered for everything in an attempt to get fixed, get healed up, equipped and ready for the call.

I didn't realise the irony of it, that my attempts to make myself ready were just another manifestation of my brokenness and I was not getting any closer to my desired goal. Ministry was another fig leaf I could hide behind impress and intimidate people with. My desire for ministry, fame and reputation was a re-enactment of Satan's own original sin of pride and ambition. The prophet Isaiah tells us that this once beautiful angel aspired to ascend and raise himself up, enthroned (Isaiah 14:12-14) above God himself. Five times we read that Satan said in his heart, "I will". In his orphaned inner being and with ambition fueled by his beauty, his gifting and position was what caused him to eventually crash and burn. Reaching the top is not necessarily God's best for you. Lucifer's story reveals a dreadful tale of the destruction wrought by selfish ambition and is a warning against pride in one's own ability.

Having been thrust into the pulpit early in my Christian life, I thought I deserved to be in a position of eminence and should be seen in the public spotlight; but Jesus did not consider position, fame or glory anything to be grasped or pursued (Philippians 2:6). Despite His exalted position and power, He brought himself low with no loftier aspirations than to know His Father and do only what he saw His Father do.

Oh, to have THAT heart within.

The call to ministry is a genuine call from the Lord, but we are filling so many people with illusions of greatness that the Lord has not called them to. we are setting them up for disappointment, burnout and even a loss of faith. I tire of hearing young people being told they have a great destiny in the Lord, that they are called to be world changers and history makers; where they are encouraged to pursue a life in ministry when it might serve them better to get a job and learn something of life that way. Sonship, being a child of God is not found in ministry, it is found in intimacy and even hiddenness. John the Baptist and Jesus both spent around thirty years in obscurity; Moses spent some years in Midian before returning to Egypt as Israel's deliverer, and David 'wasted' over twenty years being misunderstood, chased from home and hunted in the desert after his anointing.

Many people are leaving ministry situations across the Western world, having entered into something without calling. Having been encouraged by 'prophetic' words and stirring altar calls, many have gone into ministry ill equipped in their inner being and disillusionment quickly replaces enthusiasm and zeal. Burnout today, I believe, is caused by entering into ministry too soon. Even though you may have a calling, to go into that calling too soon can be disastrous and even destroy future ministry.

The call of God is something internal, a dialogue between Father and child. It is not something that comes through an altar call or a prophetic word or a school of ministry certificate. These things can confirm a true calling, but they can never create that call for you. We are creating a generation of believers who become disappointed when the promise does not quickly appear. I've seen selfish ambition in my own heart, and I see it throughout the body of Christ. The desire for reputation, acclaim and promotion within Christian structures where we give ourselves grandiose titles and positions merely feeds a deep need in the orphan heart for recognition, affirmation and acceptance that truly only comes from Father's ongoing impartation of life.

It often causes the baser instincts of mankind to manifest in our behaviour and has left me feeling sullied and cheapened when I have sunk to those levels. At times it sounds as though ministry, in some circles, is being presented in the way that Paul spoke of in 1Timothy 6:5 *"…men of corrupt mind, who have been robbed of the truth and who think that godliness is a means to financial gain."*

I do not want my life to be like that.

Crete 1984

GOODBYE TO AMBITION

I read a statement by someone speaking about their pursuit of miracles and manifestation of God's power and he said, "The Path to power is intimacy with God". While there may be some kind of truth to that statement, I found myself in profound disagreement with it. It propagates the erroneous idea that God is a slot machine and we use Him for our own ends; just get the recipe right and everything else will automatically follow on. It saddens me that we have reduced relationship with God, to a formula from which, if followed correctly, we will reap.

The desire for power and miraculous manifestations is, I believe, merely a symptom of our desire for recognition and affirmation. It is a result of mankind losing connection with love. The love deficit we experience in our beings, we attempt to comfort through performance and achievement.

It is important for us to understand that power does

not equal godliness – look at the Corinthian church. They saw power, gifts manifested yet everyone's selfish ambition for prominence and recognition resulted in strife, cliques, sexual immorality, greed and confusion. We read the bible passages speaking of God's power and desire to be the man or woman of God, doing wonderful things but the desire for His power can be a corrupting influence; just read the sad tale of Simon Magus in the Book of Acts (Acts 8:4-24) to realise the truth of that.

One thing I have learned about power and reputation is, that it is temporal. All of these titles and gifts will, one day, be done away with; 1 Corinthians 15:24 *The end will come, when he hands over the kingdom to God the Father after he has destroyed all dominion, authority and power.* There will come a day when there are no Apostles, Prophets, worship leaders or any other titles and giftings. They will no longer be necessary for the perfect will have come (1 Cor.13:10).

If these things have become the focus of our energy and even our identity, what will we be when they are no more? Having spent so much time and effort building our reputations, ministries and place in the body, having established our identities as men and women of God, what are we when all of that is stripped away and we are left with only me? The problem many of us, in the body of Christ, face is that we have no idea who we are and so seek acclamation through performance. Possessing the language of sonship does not equate to living in sonship.

If we only see intimacy with God as a means to an end, then we are not truly experiencing intimacy with Him. When we seek relationship with anyone based on what we can get out of it – based on what they can offer us and how it will give us a boost or promote our reputation then we are using them. Seeking a pathway to power by '*using*' God our Father will not bring satisfaction. The search for satisfaction, the heart cry for true intimacy to know and be known will not be quieted by gifts, miracles and performance.

Intimacy is not a means to an end; it is not the pathway to power - intimacy itself is the end, it is the goal! God the Father's desire is to draw you and me into a place of harmonious relationship. That's what it means to walk like Jesus, because Jesus lived as a son to His Father in harmonious relationship. Doing great deeds is not walking as Jesus walked – it is merely trying to do the things Jesus did. The things He did flowed from His relationship with Father (John 5:19).

Living like Jesus isn't something we do; it is something Father does in us as He pours love into our lives. As His love touches the orphan issues of our hearts, the wounds and love deficits which drive ambition and desire for reputation, we begin to be aware that there is another way. Surrendering to love and to intimacy may not seem spectacular but it is a deeper, longer lasting and definitely more fulfilling path to follow.

Love poured into our hearts brings a whole new perspective on ministry so that we begin to see it as a privilege and honour rather than a means of elevating us to some exalted high place. Love enlightens the eyes of our heart to see Him as He really is and the true hope to which He has called us, the glorious inheritance we share with all of the saints.

Ministry is intended to be a manifestation of his love, and any ministry that is not a manifestation of love is not being directed by God's Spirit. I do not mean our own human efforts at being loving people, which ebbs and flows with our moods and will; but love that becomes our source of life, sustaining and energising us from the core of our being; love that has been poured into us by God Himself and found a resting place in our hearts.

Love that finds its source within a human being is not true love. It is merely the effort and activity of a man or woman attempting to present themselves as something they are not. I don't care how many spectacular results we see. If the love which is sourced only in the Father, is not being manifested then we need to rethink what we are doing and how we are doing it.

Perhaps while we are caught up in our own self-importance, knowledge and ambition (Matthew 11:25, 26), we become blinded to the reality of God as our Father in any real and meaningful way. Some may even scoff at the idea of God being a loving Father, while holding to the doctrine of it, preferring instead to relate to the judge and furious punisher of humanity.

In Ephesians chapter one, Paul begins by saying that we need *"the God of our Lord Jesus Christ, the glorious Father,* [to] *give you the Spirit of wisdom and revelation, so that you may know Him better."* Paul writes this to born again, Spirit filled Christians and tells them they don't know God the glorious Father well enough to understand His purposes for us as individuals and as a family so he prays that the Father Himself would change that through His wisdom and revelation of Himself to us.

As we begin to understand who Father really is, then His love poured into our heart enlightens the eyes of our heart to understand what His calling is really all about - and it is not about fulfilling our selfish ambition for recognition and personal gain.

That is what lies behind the schools we operate, the desire to create a space and time for individuals where Father would impart that revelation to our hearts, and we would begin to understand who He is and the substance of His love.

Love is what we were made for.

Living loved is not about having a singular experience of God, like a photograph that we can put in our wallet. It is an ongoing, unfolding of the depths of His heart and being, a revealing of His truest nature as a Father who loves us. It is only possible for this to happen as we learn to lay aside our ambitions and desire for prominence. Otherwise, the eyes of our heart remain unenlightened. Still in darkness, we are unable to see the hope and the riches of our true inheritance among the saints in Christ Jesus and we miss the true purpose of Jesus' life, death and resurrection. All of which were designed to bring us back to the garden experience of being loved by Father.

London 1990

CHAPTER 8

MADE FOR LOVE

Despite the internal trauma of family life, other than the bullying which began when I was around nine or ten years old, I lived a relatively innocent existence during my early years. There were external traumas, like the time I fell from a tree swing and landed in the middle of the river cart running through Pollok Country Park or the incident when older boys held me down while a younger boy bit me on the back, and the embarrassment of having to wear my mum's clothes to school (not her dresses obviously) with wellington boots.

Being Celebrated, Norfolk, Virginia

After my dad's death, I began to hang around with riskier company and, in addition to the regular fights I began to get involved in, by the time I was twelve or thirteen years old, I had knives held to my throat on three separate occasions. In one instance where I was allowed to go into the city centre on my own, as I stood at the bus stop on my way back home, I saw a crowd of older boys chasing another one. As he ran past the bus stop, he grabbed me and held a black handled stiletto knife at my throat shouting at people to help him. I don't recall all of the details, but an older man managed to get me free and the boy ran off again.

Another incident occurred as I was walking home from school and two older boys whom I did not know confronted me. They were looking for someone I had never heard of, and when I told them this, they pulled out a large kitchen knife and began threatening me. Somehow, I managed to talk my way out of them cutting me and stealing my money.

The other occasion was during my first year in high school. I visited a friend who lived in another gang territory and when his brother's friend found out where I lived, he came at me with a large butcher knife. Thankfully, my friend's brother stopped him.

At school, gang wars would erupt with older teenage boys producing knives, axes, chains and on occasion, swords in the playground. I tried to stay cool, but it was terrifying to a twelve-year-old. I saw and engaged in huge gang fights, in school and in the streets, where weapons were regularly brandished and used. At seventeen, I was stabbed and lost my teeth during an attack in the city centre, that was only halted by the actions of a passing taxicab driver. On other occasions, my shoulder was violently dislocated in a fight and my ear was sliced open by an older boy as we fought. I recall the blood spraying up the wall of our sitting room whenever I shook my head.

Many other vicious incidents took place, too many to recount here, but it is fair to say my growing years were not peaceful nor without drama. These experiences (and many others) left me feeling as though I didn't belong or fit in, feeling afraid that I was not like others. I have since realised that fear was a constant in my life. I had thought fear entered my life when I had so many scary experiences, but I was reminded during writing this of an experience I had while on retreat. During a meeting, I had a vision of myself in the womb, but I was agitated and anxious. The reason for my agitation being that I did not feel safe. The world outside seemed dangerous for me and I didn't want to be born into it.

This was the basis of fear and anxiety in my life – everything built on this foundation. Shame was an ever-present shadow, and one of the consequences was that it left me with a shyness and awkwardness towards girls where romance was concerned. I can still remember my first steps into the world of dating. I asked a girl at the same primary school as me to go to the cinema. We arranged to meet, but she never showed up. That made me even more reticent to approach girls on a romantic level. There were a number of incidents over the years that left me feeling humiliated in my attempts at romance or where I found myself replaced by someone else in a girlfriend's affections. Many years later, I recall one girl telling me, *"John, you would have so many more girlfriends if you would just stop being their friend."*

Between my dad's death and my lack of success in romance, by the time I was sixteen, I determined never to get attached to anyone ever again. I concluded that they would leave too and in order to avoid that pain, I closed my heart to any attachments. I learned to cover my brokenness and exert some control in my life and those around me. Life could not have been easy for those closest to me, especially my wife as she was exposed to this part of my personality.

The problem was that I had no idea I was controlling or broken to the extent that it made life miserable for others. I had developed and finely tuned my ability to manipulate and control people in ways that made me feel safe and secure. It also helped to keep people at a distance emotionally. I had no idea the damage I was doing. As a friend is wont to say, *"You don't know what you don't know."* I did not understand that the times I sensed distance between Fiona and me was not her fault. She was reacting to me pushing her away and rejecting her attempts at loving me, so our conversation felt as though it was focussed on her work and friends rather than about her inner life, which I didn't know how to discuss anyway.

We spoke little of what was happening in our internal world, in our hearts. For Fiona, I had pushed away from that kind of intimacy and she felt as though I wouldn't hear her. For me, I didn't want anyone to see into that place of intimacy where I hid my fears, wounds, insecurities and feelings of inadequacy and it made me self-righteous, inflexible, demanding, judgmental and critical.

When I became a believer, I created a fig leaf of godliness and righteousness to justify my behaviour, my unyielding and inflexible character and personality. I could quote chapter and verse to justify my unyielding and intransigent behaviour. But underneath, all of the trauma and wounding, I had suppressed, continued to push through and hurt others around me.

I was the only one who couldn't see it.

My wife loved me very much, but I didn't know love. I didn't know how to receive it and I didn't know how to give it. Fiona had no idea what she did wrong (nothing by the way) and was hurt and confused by my reaction. I had no concept of love or how to deal with it. Intimacy felt like an invasion and put me under threat of becoming vulnerable and I had worked hard at not being vulnerable, so I pushed against love and intimacy even while declaring my love for Fiona. I really cannot express the depth of my gratitude to, and the extent of my admiration for her, in sticking with me (at the time of writing we have recently celebrated our thirty third wedding anniversary).

There were good times too and Fiona's love, along with a measure of healing in ministry times, enabled me to begin to receive love and even give it to some degree. It remained selfish and egocentric on my part though; it was still all about me and my needs as I tried to find people or things that would fill a bottomless pit of lovelessness in my heart while being unable to give much in return. When I was exposed to this new perspective in the revelation of Father's Love, I was brought face to face with many of the issues of my heart.

I began to see and address some of these issues following the time in Toronto; and I experienced a level of freedom and ability to receive love that I had thought was beyond me. Father began to minister to my wounds and the loveless areas of my heart. Often, I would find myself crying with no idea why until the Lord told me it was Him ministering to the wounds of my heart, wounds I was unaware of and had no clue as to what He was healing.

The wonderful thing in this revelation is that love never stops pouring into our lives and our hearts, but the scary thing is that we can harden our hearts against love and remain totally unaffected by it. Father is moving through my history with the scars of the past being exposed to His love as I refuse to harden my heart any longer. A refusal to harden my heart has been key to receiving greater measures of love. Not only to receive but also to contain love to the degree that it influences my internal life.

I had not known that my inability to love and be loved was because I had hardened my heart. I thought a hardened heart was that of a really wicked person whose sins had inured them to shame and guilt. BUT I now understand that a hardened heart is one that has been closed as defense against pain. My inability to know love – even the love of God himself – was due to my fear of being hurt ever again.

I was familiar with scoffing and cynicism, sarcasm and skepticism, but had never understood that these things were hardening agents acting upon my heart so that eventually I was unable to respond from my heart. I could respond or act out of my intellect, my will and even my emotions but they are not the same as a heart response. I had shut away the core of my being to protect it from wounding but all I really did was to construct a prison for myself.

In order to receive love in the measure He intends, I am learning not to live with those qualities, those hardening agents and generally, I am improving in that area. Love is beginning to find a dwelling place within my being and my heart is starting to emerge from its cage.

The transformation, and realisation, of this revelation

was smoother and less painful for Fiona, but both of us are walking together as he continues to delve into the depths of our hearts with his love.

Mum & Dad

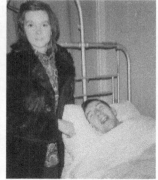

Mum & Dad, Hospital 1970s

1961

With my siblings

My maternal Grandmother

1963 / 1964

School Photograph

Glasgow 1990s

Ordination, 2008

With my mum

Wedding Day with my Grandmothers

Lake Zurich 1992

Turkey 1995

My Favourite Women

CHAPTER 9

A HARDENED HEART

When people speak of opening our hearts to Father, I now think of the deliberate decision to not accommodate cynicism, sarcasm, etc. I had spent most of my life hardening my heart and resisting love, and as His love continues to soften me and heal my pain, I am discovering what I lost out on during those years.

I catch myself, at times, leaning towards those heart attitudes whenever tenderness is demonstrated, or kindness is shown. It may only be on a television programme or  a moment in life, but I can feel the activity of those hardening agents on my heart, and it is a deliberate decision by me to allow tenderness and kindness to affect and influence me. Tenderness and kindness are sometimes uncomfortable experiences for my heart, but love has shown me the good that they create in me.

How did I get to that place? I was wrestling on and off with how to open my heart. I was trying to find the key or method and formula. That is how I had always approached the things of God, breaking them down into a method.

Throughout my life the idea of an open heart has been a completely foreign idea to me. For most of my life I have not had an open heart, although I have only come to that understanding in the last number of years. From early childhood, I never made connections, never lived in affectionate relationships. My mum and dad loved me, but they were unable to express it in terms that I understood. They were not expressively affectionate, so I didn't grow up with the experience of affection and quality time.

As I got older, one of the results of this was that romantic relationships really only equated to sex. I needed affection. I needed to have that expressed but it wasn't happening in ANY sphere of my life except during sex – when I was, generally, in control. To protect myself so that I would not be hurt, I became someone who was never wrong, never sorry, and everyone else was an idiot. I acted tough and pretended not to be afraid. This was my armour, my protection. In protecting myself, I didn't realise my emotional responses had been inhibited, and I formed a heart of stone within me – a heart unresponsive, incapable of responding. Such a heart cannot be penetrated, even by love, and it becomes a trap for its owner. No matter how much I wanted to respond with love, with affection and tenderness, I was unable to.

I wanted to speak tenderly but ended up shouting and being scathing or angry. When I read the Bible about love it was a concept, a doctrine and theology. The idea of actually experiencing Love was so far removed from my experience and when I saw or was offered tenderness, I resisted it, pushed it away. What I was doing was hardening my heart.

The Bible tells us in Proverbs 4:23-24, *"Above all else, guard your heart, for it is the wellspring of life. Put away perversity from your mouth; keep corrupt talk far from your lips."*

I believe that what the Bible is saying is these things; perversity of mouth and corrupt speech, come from hardened hearts. It is the hardening of our hearts that 'protects' us from love. This hardening makes it difficult to hear tenderness and love so that we relate to God by way of commands and laws rather than conversation and intimacy. Often, we then relate to people with anger, judgement and control.

Exodus Chapters 7 and 8 tells us five times that pharaoh's heart was hardened, and *he did not listen*. Hardening our hearts is a persistent rejection of love to the point that we eventually become deaf to love's call when it is offered. That is a frightening reality. We can be so intent on protecting ourselves from wounding that we miss the very love which heals our wounds.

Mark 6:51-52 tells us, "...*he got into the boat with them, and the wind ceased. And they were utterly astounded, for they did not understand about the loaves, but their **hearts were hardened**.*"

A hardened heart leads to a lack of understanding about the things of God. When we have lost that true understanding, we turn to our intellect and concoct explanations from our paucity of experience. Sadly, my observation is that this is the foundation of much of modern Christianity. Our thinking on God is built upon intellectual explanations and accumulation of information because of the general lack of experiencing Him as Father. The Church father Augustine said that if we have understood, then what we have understood is not God. I 'understood' God, but I did not know Him as He truly is. I am so glad He never gave up and I have begun to experience Him beyond the accumulation of knowledge about Him.

In Hebrews 3:7 through Hebrews 4:7, the writer gives us an insight into the importance of this issue *Therefore, as the Holy Spirit says, "Today, if you hear his voice, do not harden your hearts as in the rebellion, on the day of testing in the wilderness, where your fathers put me to the test and saw my works for forty years.*

*...Exhort one another every day, as long as it is called "today,"
that none of you may be hardened by the deceitfulness of sin.
As it is said, "Today, if you hear his voice, do not harden your
hearts as in the rebellion."*

*His works were finished from the foundation of the world.
For he has somewhere spoken of the seventh day in this way:
"And God rested on the seventh day from all his works." And
again, in this passage he said, "They shall not enter my rest."*

*...Again, he appoints a certain day, "Today," saying through
David so long afterward, in the words already quoted, "Today,
if you hear his voice, do not harden your hearts."*

Hardening our hearts in accordance with the cynicism
and heartlessness of this world leads to people who are
devoid of love, devoid of the ability to hear God's tender
voice and who lack real understanding of him and his true
ways. Perhaps this goes partway to explaining the shallow-
ness of some of our Christian living and is why Paul prays
as he does in the first chapter of Ephesians. Even in Paul's
day, many early believers' hearts were unaccustomed to the
tenderness of love.

I believe scripture is saying that the way to guard your
heart is to not harden it. From my own experience, I see how
I hardened (and can still harden) my heart at times. 'Seeing'

these scriptures about hardening was so helpful to me, but it didn't tell me how to open my heart. The only reference I can find in the Bible to a human being opening their heart is in 2 Corinthians 6:11-13: *"We have spoken freely to you, Corinthians; our heart is wide open. You are not restricted by us, but you are restricted in your own affections. In return (I speak as to children) widen* (or open) *your hearts also."*

But it doesn't tell us how to open our heart, and this frustrated me. I wanted the formula! I continued to be frustrated until one day I read a few words in the book of Acts for, perhaps, the hundredth time. In Acts 16:14, we read that *"One of those listening was a woman named Lydia, a dealer in purple cloth from the city of Thyatira, who was a worshiper of God. The Lord opened her heart to respond to Paul's message."* As Lydia listened to Paul's preaching, in contrast to Pharaoh, she refused to harden her heart against what was being said, creating the opportunity for God himself to open her heart to hear what he was saying to her through Paul's preaching.

When I read that, it became wonderful news. I understood that it is not my responsibility to open my heart. I no longer feel responsible for that aspect of life, which is a huge relief because the truth is, I don't know how. I am learning how to not harden my heart and create opportunity for the Lord to open my heart more widely to His love. I am discovering that it is the entrance of His love that is transforming my life, not the knowledge of it or the doctrine of it but the receiving of loves substance, in the depths of my being.

At the end of 2007, Fiona and I felt to spend some time in prayer about the future. As we did, I increasingly felt that I should leave my pastoral position with a local Pentecostal church. After Christmas of 2007, I spoke with the deacons, asking them to pray and see if the Lord was also speaking to them about this. With regret, they came back to us saying that they did think this was the Lord, and though they did not want to see us go, we agreed a timescale for our departure.

We made things known to the church in May of 2008 (ironically just after my ordination ceremony) and began preparing them for our departure. My last Sunday as pastor of that church was August 18, 2008. I'm not sure what I was expecting, but I thought my denomination would come up with offers and when that did not materialise, I began looking for regular employment, which also did not materialise.

During the three years since we had attended that month-long school at Toronto Airport Church and my departure as pastor, I had connected with Fatherheart Ministries more and thought that this must be the door opening, but no letter came from New Zealand either. I was confused and more than a little irritated with God. Ministry was still a fig leaf I wore but now the Lord wanted to deal with it.

I railed against this situation with constant complaints to Father. *"Haven't you called me and destined me for great things? Where is the breakthrough, the promotion? Why can't I find a job?"* Something was definitely wrong. I thought perhaps I needed to war against the principalities and powers which were so obviously opposing me and obstructing the Lord's great plans for me. I would have to fast and pray against these fiendish schemes of the enemy. One day Fiona told me she had been praying and heard Father say that He didn't want me to work. I instantly knew she had heard wrong. Of course, God wants a man to work and earn his own bread, be independent and strong.

I can hear you laughing. As I went to Father to speak to Him about this, He clearly told me my wife was correct and that I needed to listen to her more. It took me all those years to learn that lesson, but I'm glad that at last I heard it.

As I spent time with Him, Father began to show me my self-righteousness, independence, pride in my own ability and my unerring sense of always being right and everyone else being wrong. He began to teach me about sonship being a life of dependence; that spiritual maturity was not growing up and learning to do it by myself. I had thought I needed to be more grown up and mature, but if I were going to be a son to Him it would be by becoming more childlike rather than more adult like.

<u>Spiritual maturity is growing down and understanding
I cannot ever do it by myself.</u>

I had spent my whole life wanting to be grown up and I
had learned to do it by myself. I didn't need to depend on
anyone else. I was capable on my own. But, if Jesus only
did what he saw Father doing, then why should I think it
would be any different for me? If it was Father in Jesus doing
His work (John 14:10), then shouldn't I expect to fulfill my
call the same way rather than ministering out of an orphan
independence? Shouldn't it be Father living in me that makes
life possible for me, too (John 14:23)?

I had lived with a dad who, from my perspective, never
gave me anything, who was unable to love me, affirm or
provide for me. I never had a dad who would come watch
me play soccer or take me to the park and kick a ball with
me. I remember feeling anger when another boy's dad came
to see him play for our soccer team and the coach would
drop me from the team to put that boy on the field instead.
That created a lot of resentment in my heart, and I regret to
say led to occasions of me bullying that boy.

I did things for my dad; as I said previously, I spoon fed
him. I brushed his teeth for him, gave him drinks etc. I
had no idea how to be fathered. I had fathered myself my
whole life.

After my dad died, my maternal grandmother was also

heavily involved in our family life, so I had two women telling me how to live when I was supposed to be the man of the house. Well, you can imagine the ruckus this caused and the resentment I built up in my heart. I became my own father and wouldn't be told by anyone what to do or how to do it.

All of this meant that when someone spoke of God being my real Dad, a Father to me, I had no concept of what that meant. When people spoke about the Father, I patronised them from a great height. I already knew that theology. I knew the doctrine and had even taught on the topic, but I had no idea what a father was or how to let anyone father me.

Somewhere around 2000, the realisation began to dawn on me that perhaps I had some issues. I attended a weekend retreat, and during the weekend some issue around my dad's death came up for me. I cannot remember what it was that surfaced, but I went into a little prayer room with one of the weekend's leaders.

He said to me, "John, it's as though there is still an eleven-year-old boy holding onto your dad. If you want to move on with God, you need to let your dad go."

I began to try and pray, but nothing would come out. I really wanted to do this, but it wouldn't happen, I could not get the words to come out of my mouth.

This man said to me, *"John, you need to let your dad go; God wants to be your Father."*

What came out of my mouth was a complete shock to me. Jesus said that out of the heart the mouth speaks. Well, words were released, and I spoke what was in my heart.

"NO, you took my dad from me, you're not taking his place!"

I was a spiritual leader, a man of God who pursued holiness and the things of God with serious passion yet here I was saying God could not be who He wanted to be in my life. For so many years, I had been warring with Him in my heart. In my heart I would not let Him be who He wanted to be to me, all of my desire for godliness, ministry and walking with God was a sham. I was quite happy to serve the Almighty, labour as a servant in His kingdom but there was a little boy who would not allow Him to be who He really is, my Father.

Eventually, I was able to pray some sort of prayer, which I have completely forgotten.

CHAPTER 10

AN OFFENDED HEART

The heart is indeed a mystery and known only by God. He had to expose me to what was really there before we could move on together. Yet, it was still another five years before I understood. None of us truly know what is happening in

our hearts, hiding behind our fig leaves of false identity, spiritual activities and firmly entrenched beliefs. Only the Lord truly knows us in our deepest being. We go through our Christian lives fervently loving God, being committed to Him, earnest in our service, our Bible knowledge and church attendance but unaware that within each of us is a little boy or girl, lurking in the depths of our hearts who is resistant, in one way or other, to God being our Father.

What is the issue in *your* heart that is blocking true intimacy with Papa?

The idea of God being a Father to us is offensive to many believers and can extract angry responses from people when confronted with the reality of His Fatherhood, or it can result in a cool dismissal of such a thing as babyish nonsense. Believing doctrine and giving intellectual assent to a theology doesn't give us the experience of truth. In fact, it can often inoculate us to the experience that our theology points to.

Many of Jesus' followers believed what He said but when it came to something outside of their worldview they balked. In the book of John, we read, *"On hearing it, many of his disciples said, "This is a hard teaching. Who can accept it?" Aware that his disciples were grumbling about this, Jesus said to them, "Does this offend you? ...He went on to say, "This is why I told you that no one can come to me unless the Father has enabled him." From this time many of his disciples turned back and no longer followed him (John 6:60, 65, 66)."*

Often, I meet people who are offended by our speaking of the Father in a personal and sometimes childlike way. Yet,

Jesus continually spoke of His Father like that. Over two hundred times in four gospels, Jesus referred to His Father in personal ways and included us in this when He spoke of Our Father (Matthew 6:9), your Father in heaven (Matthew 5:16, 45; 6:1, 32; 9; 7:11; Mark 11:25; Luke 11:13) and other instances. Why does this offend us, when Jesus told us about the depth of His Father's affection and concern for each of us? Why cannot we come as little children dependent upon a big Father who knows what we need and is pleased to give it to us as a gift of love?

Is it that we have become so puffed up with our own importance and reputations that we can no longer see the reality many of our doctrines and theologies point to (Matthew 11:25)?

I had built a life of always being right, always knowing and pontificating about what I knew in order to impress and intimidate others, keeping them from discovering I was not what I purported to be. In truth, it was smoke and mirrors. My preaching about God and especially of Him as a Father was not based on my experience of being fathered by Him. It was merely intellectual information I had accumulated and formed into a teaching.

I was so far away from knowing God being a Father to me (2 Corinthians 6:18) until I met James and Denise Jordan and heard Father speak to me about my identity. When I came to the period of inactivity that began in August 2008, I did not think it was God Himself who had brought me to it, until my wife shared what he had spoken to her. My wife speaking up helped me into a place where my heart could hear something that was outside of my thinking and understanding, beyond my worldview.

So much of what Father is speaking to the world is outside of our thinking and understanding, that's why we can't always hear Him. Some of what He says is beyond our experience and is outside of the belief system we have constructed for ourselves. Our insistence on being right and clinging to our beliefs is rendering us deaf to His voice. In our pride and certainty, **we have hardened our hearts**.

When we were ignorant of Him, living a life outside of Christ, He was speaking to each of us, but we were not able to hear His voice. When I came to salvation in 1985, it was the result of God reaching out to me, speaking to me over the course of my life but it took me twenty-four years to hear Him. It took another twenty years to be able to hear Him speak to me about being my Father.

I was taught and had held to a false belief that before we came to Christ, God was not involved in our lives, that He was unable to look at us because of our sins. Today I have discovered this is simply not true. Indeed, it is He who loved us so much that He gave his son (John 3:16,17) to show the world who He is and lead us to Him.

The writer of Proverbs tells us, *"The eyes of the Lord are everywhere, keeping watch on the wicked and the good"* (Prov.15:3). I guess as He keeps watch he must see 'sinners' engaging in sin and does not turn away in disgust nor is He breathing fire and threatening lightning bolts from heaven.

When Jesus walked the earth, He engaged regularly with 'sinners', eating and drinking with them, doing life with them, which caused Him to draw much criticism from the religious establishment, but He didn't appear to be bothered by it. Incredibly, He appears to have remained uncontaminated by the experience. Remember Jesus only does what he sees Father doing. His interaction with 'sinners' was because that is what He saw His Father doing. Almighty God, Jehovah, is actively involved in the lives of frail and sinful human beings.

God is unable to be influenced by or affected in any way whatsoever by sin. That's what it means for Him to be holy. It's why He was able to patiently pursue me in my younger years and why He could call my name and wait for me to respond many years later.

When man sinned in Eden, his Father did not turn from him but embraced him in order to cloak him with the skins of the first sacrifice, just as he covers us in Jesus today. He touched the 'sinner', engaged with him, even after the man refused to accept responsibility for what he had done. God is not keeping His distance from mankind but is deeply involved and actively seeking to draw every human being to Himself through Jesus. People in this world, believers included, have God encounters every day but are too often unaware that it is He they are being touched by.

The revelation of Father's love is not confined to church or to Christian believers. It is His desire for the whole world to know who He is and experience His loving embrace (1 John 2:2; Jeremiah 3:19). The arts world often plugs into spiritual realities without understanding what they are seeing. The creative process and creative inspiration can be a spiritual state without the person being religious in any way. Many of the movies we watch today carry the theme of a father's relationship with his children.

Think of Liam Neeson in *Taken* or Mel Gibson in *What Women Want* and *Blood Father*; Albert Finney's performance in *Big Fish* or Denis Quaid in *The Day After Tomorrow*; Kurt Russell's recent role in *Guardians of the Galaxy (Pt.2)* and Channing Tatum in *White House Down*.

There are so many other movies carrying this as a major theme or a significant subplot. This is what the Father of Jesus, our Papa, is doing in the world today. My personal favourite is the story of a little boy who disobeys his dad and is captured, taken far away and held prisoner. The story is of his dad's journey and struggle to bring him home. It is the gospel in one hundred minutes by Disney and is of course, 'Finding Nemo'.

This is not 'new'; God has been doing this since the 1970s. I remember Television shows, such as *Father, dear, Father* with Patrick Cargill and later programmes such as *The Cosby Show* and *The Prince of Bel Air*. Now we have Homer in *The Simpsons*' and Peter in *Family Guy*. *NCIS* had the running theme through many series of the individual characters' complicated relationship with their dads.

There are many songs around this theme too, James Grant's *My Father's Coat*; Glasvegas' *Daddy's Gone*; Cat Stevens' *Father and Son*; Beyoncé *Daddy*; Bruce Springsteen *My Father's Eyes*; Jason Blaine *Dance With My Daughter*; Luther Vandross *Dance with my Father*; Temptations *Papa Was A Rolling Stone*; Johnny Cash *A Boy Named Sue* and many more. The world hears God, but they don't know it is Him speaking about being a Father to them.

Do we really know all there is to God to such a degree that we can dismiss Jesus' emphasis on God as Abba, Papa? How can the church bring the world to an understanding of truth and the experience of reconciliation (2 Corinthians 5:19), when so many of us are offended by the concept of God as a loving Father who invites us to know Him as Papa rather than master? How can we lead the world to understanding when we are not experiencing Him "*being a Father to us*" (2 Corinthians 6:18a) for ourselves?

Jesus' whole ministry was about reconnecting humanity to their Father, the one who breathed His own breath into them and has spent thousands of years preparing and calling for their return, for them to come home to Him. It is God's greatest wish that each person on the planet would experience His love, and it is when we experience love, not when we acquire information about it, that love effects its power of transformation upon our souls.

Perhaps the problem with modern Christianity is similar to that of ancient Pharisees, we have constructed systems devoid of the experience of love while preaching about it. We have defined to the 'nth' degree what religion is but have forgotten what the reality of it feels like within our hearts.

CHAPTER 11

NEEDING A FIX

Towards the end of 2013, someone hurt me deeply, and I crashed. The carefully crafted image of holiness and my fig leaves of competence and capability were no longer sufficient. I began to notice  new behaviour patterns and when I mentioned to my wife that I was noticing a change in my behaviour, she gave me a look that said, "*You've always been like that.*" Then, in case I hadn't gotten the message, she told me, "*You've always been that way.*"

I became aware of anxiety gnawing away at me inside, and a depressive feeling seemed to come over me. I know now that these were things that had always been there, but I had ignored them and covered them up. I fell back into the pattern of thinking that I need to be fixed, so Fiona accompanied me to therapy with a lady who had been recommended by a friend. It turned out quite differently to what I expected. Instead of fixing me, God used the therapist to pick apart my life.

During the sessions there were times that little boy whose dad had died would manifest, like he just walked into the room and took over. I would become sullen, uncooperative and very defensive, resistant to all attempts to draw me out. I felt under threat. I felt accused and blamed for everything, and I felt unsafe in these situations so retreated into a defensive mentality. Over time I began to see some of the life patterns I had developed and hidden in, keeping everyone out. These sessions lasted a couple of months, and I eventually visited the doctor in October 2013. I was prescribed medication (which I am still taking) for anxiety and mild mood disorder. It was a real inner struggle to accept the necessity of being medicated.

After a while, I decided to see another therapist. This time I chose, quite deliberately, to see a man. I had spent my whole life unable to really relate to men. I found it easier and safer to relate to women. I abhorred the rough way of speaking, the uncouth and base conversation topics amongst men. Of course, I never betrayed this feeling publicly but tried my best to fit in and I'm sure I fooled a good number of people with my talk and behaviour. Even though I never felt like it I gave people the impression of being "one of the boys."

I deliberately decided to break with my safe options and chose to go to a male therapist. For eight months or so, I would regularly spend an hour with Alan as we explored my stuff. He was a gentle and sensitive guy, and over time, I found myself becoming more open with him than I had ever been with another man. Initially, my intent was to discover the root cause of my depression, fear and anxiety and to uncover why I had developed certain behaviour patterns and control issues. I figured if we got to those things, then Father could pour His love in to that place and I would be healed, free from my stuff; be fixed!

Therapy was still about being 'fixed' so I could be a better man of God, more effective in communicating His love and possibly even more successful. How God must have laughed! As we progressed over many weeks, I began to understand that much of my life and the way I had conducted myself in it was due to the traumatic experiences that I wrote of in earlier chapters, and I had accepted these experiences as normal life without ever processing or addressing them in any way.

Trauma puts us in a position where our decision-making abilities are affected, and we are more susceptible to 'winds and currents' of other peoples' influence. My decisions and choices were influenced by what others had done to me, and I lived in response to that.

Everyone lives their life in response to something – the need for acceptance, the pressure to succeed or the desire for wealth, etc. Love and affection were not an ongoing part of my experience growing up, instead my overwhelming experience was trauma and the choices I made, the way I responded to people and situations, were determined by this trauma and my life.

I lived in response to trauma and fear rather than in response to love.

In therapy, I found that everything I had experienced and had buried was still there; the shame, violence and pain, humiliation, all unprocessed and influencing how I lived my life. The issues I was facing, the anxiety and mood problems, were not the result of my recent hurt, rather they were the result of years of traumatic experiences. Some of which were extremely violent. The recent hurt had merely been the last straw, the catalyst for exposing my brokenness.

After all these years and all of my carefully crafted fig leaves, I was exposed and vulnerable, facing the pain I had buried. Father's Love, poured into my wounded heart, was the answer. All I needed was to expose those wounds and He would heal them. Simple, right? I had once again fallen into the trap of believing God has a magic wand He waves, and in an instant, everything is changed and made 'all better'.

I've heard people make silly comments like, "*You need a*

daddy hug or a mummy hug," but the transforming power of love is not a little pill to take as a cure all for what ails us. If it were that simple, there would be lots less pain and struggle in our lives. Through books, songs and preaching, we have been given the impression that all we need is more faith, a greater anointing and impartation from the man or woman of God. Come for the altar call, get an impartation and have the Lord take it all away; or we need to read our Bibles more, pray more, believe more and of course, attend more meetings. I have real issues with that type of Christianity. It leads people in their desperation to do silly things and fall for the possibility of being manipulated by unscrupulous people. It creates unrealistic expectations of God and of ministry and ultimately leads to disappointment and disillusionment.

Ministry is not a magic bullet. Love is the answer, but it is not a recipe to be cooked up. Love is something that is given and received in relationship over long periods of time, not a remedy to be taken twice a day like cough mixture.

I do not have any real memories of receiving love as a little boy in a way that was meaningful to me. My mum and dad loved me with everything they had, but the way they communicated love was not sufficient for my needs. Their love language was not the same language I spoke or understood. My love language is quality time, but this was not possible given our family situation, so the message communicated to me was that I was not loved (it was not true, but it was my perception).

Recently, in a conversation with my mum, she expressed her regret at being unable to spend quality time individually with each of her children and it gave me greater insight into how my parents felt during these times. We never stop to think about their emotions, feelings and thoughts during our experiences – we can become so self centred that what others feel does not matter to us at all.

The lack of quality time had a profound effect on me. Child psychologists say that this lack actually produces trauma in a child as much as violence does. Love isn't only communicated directly but babies and children learn about love as they observe it shared by the significant people in their lives. When a child sees mum and dad loving one another, embracing, kissing and speaking kindly to one another, they learn about love and actually, indirectly, receive the love that is being shared.

This demonstration of love wasn't possible in my family situation as my father's health deteriorated and all of my mum's efforts went into holding everything together. When life is like that, there is no energy left for intimacy, love, tenderness and quality attention to relationships; everyone suffers. My trauma was not only the result of anger, violence, alcohol and loss but also the absence of love communicated in a way that I could receive it. It was the result of not knowing that none of it was my fault; of the world being a confusing and frightening place for a small boy and no one explaining that to him.

The biggest impact on my life was my dad's death while he was in hospital. This was further compounded when my siblings and I were sent to live with a cousin for a few days until it was all over. Troubled by it, I built up such reserves of resentment, as this seemed to confirm my blame in it all. Growing up, I had no thought for what was happening to my parents or my siblings. My world was all about me and what I was going through. I discovered the reality of these things in the therapy sessions. As they tumbled into my consciousness, I felt completely overwhelmed by the understanding of how I had been living my life.

I had understood much of the teaching about brokenness and fig leaves as I ministered to others over the years, but here I was, having to face the reality of it in my own life. My understanding didn't help me one little bit. My heart was making known its hidden pain, and it was uncomfortable and difficult to acknowledge my weakness, my inability to cope and my complete lack of competency and capability because these had become the pillars of life for me.

As I began to speak with Father about all of this, I was shocked to discover He was not interested in fixing me. I didn't like the idea of taking medication and being dependent on pills, I was a man of God and should have faith for my deliverance and healing. But that was not in his thinking at all. Plenty of people appear to be fixed and faith filled, yet also devoid of love. I had lived that way for many years, appearing to have it together, but seriously lacking in the one thing that makes the true difference. What Father wanted for me to experience was love, specifically His nurturing love and comfort.

'Fixing' me would have bolstered what pride I had in my godliness, my own competence and faith. That was the last thing I needed. When you think about it, it makes perfect sense. If nurturing love was what I had missed out on, if comfort was what was lacking then, what I needed was not 'fixing', whatever that actually is. I needed nurturing love and comfort to fill the void in my heart. That kind of love is not an overnight solution.

If a child learns about love over many years of interactive relationship (touch, affirming words, eye contact, demonstrations of affection), why would it be any different with God our Father? His intention is that we would experience His love over a lifetime of personal and intimate interaction where we stop hardening our hearts and He pours His love into an increasingly tender heart. He doesn't want us to see Him as the kind of Father who stands at a distance, dispensing His gifts and wares, uninvolved, imparting love from a far-off place way up in the sky.

That has never been His intention for us. When God created the world, He spoke it all into being (Genesis 1:3-25) and declared it good (perfect, bountiful, prosperous). However, when it came to man, God took an entirely different approach. He modelled and shaped the man from the earth as a potter shapes clay, and blew into the man's nostrils, so the man became a breathing soul.

The breath that the man drew came from God himself. Something of the divine being was imparted into the man and thus he was in the image of God, who was his Father (Luke 3:38).

God is a Father, not because His fatherhood is male. He is the initiator of life. He not only imparts that life at conception but throughout the days of His children's existence. This up close and personal interaction at the man's 'birth' is the mark of God's intended relationship with all of mankind. It has always been His desire to personally interact with His children, in other words, to 'be a Father to them' (Jeremiah 3:19; 2 Corinthians 6:18). God's relationship with this being was, and is still, unique in all of creation.

If this is the blueprint for mankind, then God is not now and has never stood at a distance while we struggle along. His desire is to love us up close and personal, so that we understand the high value He places on each one of us, and the deep affection He has always held for us.

For many people our experience of fathers has not been like that and we find it difficult to envision God behaving that way toward us. As a result, we create religious systems based upon our ability to act that regulate our spiritual lives with behaviours and rules totally devoid of love. I lived my life as a believer within the construct of these systems and, quite honestly, it exhausted me. It was the perfect system for someone locked into my way of life, who needed something that would affirm and recognise me for my performance. The system elevated me above poorer performers, but ultimately it destroys true spirituality and makes Pharisees of us all.

The experience of Father's love for me is a real, ongoing wonder in my life. Father is constantly communing (and sometimes speaking), but I had no idea how to let Him be Father and do the things a father is supposed to do, even though I wanted it. I was walking in revelation, had begun travelling with Fatherheart Ministries sharing the revelation of Father's Love around the world, but I still had not fully understood what it meant for Him to be a father to me.

When I saw his relationship and unique dealings with man in the garden, I understood that He was not standing at a distance, I WAS. The little boy whose heart cried out, *"No, you took my dad from me,"* was still alive and kicking.

Still more comfortable in religion than relationship. Like Adam hidden among the trees afraid of his father's anger, I was hiding behind fig leaves of religion and performance out of fear. I worried that if I got too near, I would find He was displeased with me, that being me was not enough and there would be nothing left for John.

For centuries, humanity has tried to box God up and explain him within religious systems, doctrines and theologies, but He continually breaks out of these confines. In our ignorance and fear, we stand by and proclaim like the Pharisees that, *"this cannot be of God."*

As I walked through these sessions talking about my life with the therapist, for the first time, I began to see how events had affected how I was living. I had lived my whole life with internal fear and turmoil, confusion and insecurity. I had spent my whole life trying to compensate for these things. In therapy, I started to understand my behaviour and my life choices. At a young age, I had rejected my parents as a source of love and comfort and had refused to make any attachments. I could walk away from relationships and friendships without any regrets or looking back. I had learned that people always leave and that caused pain, so I avoided attachment and dependency.

I learned to hide brokenness, cover it with competency and capability. But the reality is competency eventually gives way. For me, as stated previously, it gave way to bouts of being 'down' or ill and when that happened shame increased because I couldn't "do it". I would blame my job, environment and others rather than my choices and I would double my efforts at being competent and independent, alternating between that and breaking down.

We all live with brokenness, and we all attempt to cover it, compensate for it and hide it from everyone else.

Initially, when I thought of being broken, I thought of what life had done and the trauma I experienced. BUT as I have been processing and walking in this, I have come to see, I'm not broken because life happened and did these things to me, my humanity itself is broken. Running through the core of every human being is a fracture that will not be fully healed until Jesus comes back. When man broke relationship in the garden, it caused his understanding of what it means to be human to fracture. He was always intended to be in intimate relationship with his Father, but he ran from that relationship in fear.

We were not meant to be human without the intimacy of our Father's Love.

Previously, man was naked with no shame (Genesis 2:25). After eating the fruit, their awareness and perception changed. When their eyes 'opened', they saw that they were naked and interpreted that as a wrong thing, experiencing shame and fear. We inherited that from them. They were no longer comfortable being who Father made them. Somehow being Adam the man and Adam the woman was wrong in their own judgment, and they were no longer worthy of enjoying Father's fellowship and love.

I had been trying to fix this sense of 'wrongness' my whole life. Now, I was finding that only the love of the Father could reach that place, and I had spent most of my life refusing to give Him access to that part of my being. I had been guarding that fractured place out of fear and shame, effectively blocking the Love I desired.

I have become absolutely convinced that the ONLY solution to this world's problems and the issues of life is FATHER'S LOVE. It isn't just that He wants to heal the wounds of my heart. In fact, I don't even believe that is His primary purpose. I am fully certain that His primary purpose in my life is to bring me to a place where I know beyond a doubt that I am loved, and love becomes a greater influence in my life than any brokenness or fracture of my soul.

His desire for my holiness is not driven by anger or wrath, but for me to know that sin has no hold over me any longer. The more love dwells in my heart, the less influence sin has over me. I'm not preaching sinless Christianity; I am speaking about an ever-increasing freedom from bondage as we become more and more like Him.

I am learning to accept that I am broken, but my Father doesn't see me from that perspective. Instead, He invites me to climb upon His shoulders and watch as he does amazing things.

I asked Father why He hadn't waved His hand and taken all the brokenness from me, and His response astounded me. Father told me He could do that, but I couldn't handle it. I had lived with this my whole life and had constructed coping mechanisms. What would I do if they were no longer necessary or not there? I could possibly lose my mind.

The whole industry that focuses on fixing Christians is not God's focus. It is no different from the secular self-help industry. God is not interested in fixing you. His interest is in loving you because true transformation takes place when we live in love (2 Corinthians 3:18). I'm not saying don't get ministry in areas of wounding but don't expect it to 'fix' you and turn you into something you are not. You will always be you. It cannot give you what is not already there, only Love can do that.

In the Garden, brokenness did not affect their status as son and daughter. It affected their ability to live in love and intimacy. It changed how they related to their Father and how they saw themselves.

Their brokenness did not have any influence upon God's love for them.

Our brokenness does not influence God in any negative way. He is not filled with fury and wrath. That is a religious lie. Nothing you do can change His love and affection for you. I have accepted my brokenness and I finally like being me. There is a fracture in my humanity that extends to every part of my being, emotionally, mentally spiritually, and there is nothing I can do about it except cover it up with pretense or, I can lay down my fig leaves and allow Love to cover me instead.

I have come to understand my attempts at compensating for my brokenness, my attempts at fixing myself and covering up so I can be useful to God, are actually counter-productive. God wants to come to me in my place of brokenness and love me right there, like He did with the man and woman when he cloaked them in the garden. Like he did with the son in Luke 15.

Human brokenness will not be fully healed until Jesus comes back, so I can let go of my efforts to get fixed and relax in Father's embrace. I can learn to live in the love that He brings to me. As I learn to live loved, how I do life becomes a response to love rather than a reaction to internal trauma or an attempt to get fixed and become useful. That is the revolution that love has created in my heart, living in response to love. There begins the freedom of the sons of God (Romans 8:20-21).

I am learning that His love will not necessarily take away the fracture at the core of my being, but His love poured into my life **does** change how I live with that brokenness. I no longer see myself as someone who has something wrong with them. I no longer pursue getting fixed. I am learning to enjoy this loving relationship for which I was created, taking my time, no longer rushing around trying to find validation. His love validates my existence and allows me to just be John.

CHAPTER 12

GIVING UP, LETTING GO

I was not exactly grateful to the person who hurt me and set me on this uncovering of my pain. Father has done wonderful things through it, but the pain and betrayal by this man was not something I enjoyed. I daydreamed about inflicting physical pain on him and hurting him as I was hurting (although he had not done me any physical harm).

I was familiar with Fatherheart Ministries (FHM) teaching on forgiveness and have benefited enormously from it. I found a freedom in it that traditional forgiveness teaching never brought me. True heart forgiveness brought me to a place of release from past hurts that I had struggled with for a long, long time.

One of the main factors of this teaching is compassion. It is key to heart forgiveness and I had experienced that compassion as I released lots of things from my past. As Father showed me things from another perspective, I understood that much of the hurt I received was never intended and in fact, He let me see the pain and struggle of others so that I no longer wanted to hold on to anger and grudges against them.

When I began the process in Toronto back in 2005, Father led me into a deep understanding of how life had affected my parents too. As children, we do not know there are things our parents or significant adults in our lives cannot do. When they cannot give you what you need emotionally, give your heart what it needs, you think it is because they don't want to. Despite all of the forgiveness I thought I had done, I found there was still anger and resentment within me. I was still looking for repayment and my heart still wanted something from those who had hurt me. My parents did not have the resources to give me what I needed, and I held a grudge about that until I began to see the truth. It isn't true that they didn't want to give me love. They were unable to express the love they did have for me in a way I understood.

I remember my mum sending me for elocution lessons[7]. I had been speaking for a long time and people understood me perfectly so why send me to school on a Saturday morning[8] to learn to do something I already knew how to do! But my mum knew what I didn't, that to spend my whole life speaking with a thick Glasgow dialect would severely hinder my opportunities in life as I got older.

I didn't see that far ahead. Speaking better made me a bully magnet; people thought we were trying to prove we were better than everybody else and took out their own fears in violence against me. In her great love for me and desire for me to have a better future, my mum sent me to those lessons, but I didn't understand.

We do the same with God. We look at many of his actions and judge them, but we are too immature and childish to understand the love behind it. In turn, we attribute anger to him, like I did with my mum, even cruelty and capriciousness.

I grew up thinking I was owed a great deal. As we say in Scotland, I had *"a chip on my shoulder"*. In other words, I believed the world owed me and everyone should be made to pay. In my desire to be repaid, I had not understood that I was asking for something no one could give me but as I

---

7. *Elocution is the skill of clear and expressive speech, distinct pronunciation and articulation*

8. *There are no school lessons in the U.K. on Saturdays*

saw what life had been like for my parents, I began to have for them.

My mum grew up the youngest in a house that included her parents, two brothers and three cousins who were taken in after the death of my mum's aunt. I can only imagine the chaos of that situation. Her dad was an angry man, whether it was because of his war service or because he was inclined that way, I have no idea. He died before I was born. In fact, both of my Grandfathers died before I had an opportunity to know them. This did not help with the lack of male influence in my life.

In addition, she was now struggling to hold her family, with a disabled husband and three young children, together. My father didn't have the ability or resources to be the father I needed him to be due to his disability. He was a young man trapped in a nightmare that robbed him of the joy of parenting his children.

I had no idea how difficult it was for them, and to be honest, I had no interest at that time, because it was all about me. As I 'saw' all of this during my time in Toronto, I eventually began to find my heart melting and becoming compassionate towards my parents. The anger and resentment toward them, which I had not even known was there, slowly receded until it was no longer present.

I knew I had finally, truly forgiven them in my heart

rather than merely going through a religious process that didn't change anything within. A system that says I must, I should, I ought to, I need to, I have to. I discovered that:

Forgiveness does not restore what is missing.

True forgiveness doesn't seek reparation from the offender.

True heart forgiveness makes room for God to give what is missing.

That is the reality of this revelation that I have experienced and am still experiencing. Divine love poured into my heart has been slowly but surely restoring to my soul the comfort and love that has been missing. It has been providing the reassurance my heart needed that being me is enough and that I am loved as me.

When we speak of his love, it is not an ethereal, somewhere in the heavens, philosophy or theological idea. His love is something of substance. I have stood in a crowded room, perhaps in conversation or simply observing what is going on around me and catching my wife's eye; I have felt her love physically in my being. An observer could not have seen that love being transmitted, but I felt it. Love has substance and while it may not be visible, it has a substantial reality that impacts its recipients, those who are love's focal point. Father's love has substance. There is an impartation from God our Father to compensate for the missing 'stuff' of love.

I walked through the process of heart forgiveness over a period of time as I finally dealt with many of the bitterness issues in my heart. But with this person who had hurt me in 2013, I had no desire to be compassionate towards them and was surprised at the depth of hatred and resentment I had. I was afraid of the desire to physically injure him. What if I met him in the street? Would it end with me being arrested for violent conduct, assault or worse? Would I end up injured?

I wrestled with this issue for many, many months, telling Father how much I didn't want to feel like this and being honest about my hatred and rage towards this person. I could not stop daydreaming of situations in which I would encounter him and 'deal' with it or thinking about what I would like to do. I could not seem to let go of the offence, pain and anger.

One day, as I was reading Matthew chapter 18, the story of the unforgiving servant, I saw something that had never occurred to me before. As I reread the story, I noticed how the king approached the situation. I already knew that he had taken account and knew exactly what his servant owed him. I knew he bore the price of the loss himself, and I already knew that the king had compassion on the servant and forgave him. But when I read it this time, I saw that the king never forgave the servant. It brought me up quite short, and Father began to speak to me about the situation I was in.

The anger and hate I felt was harming me greatly, disturbing my sleep and robbing me of peace (like the servant being tormented). Let's look at the verse that struck me.

The servant's master took pity on him, cancelled the debt and let him go (Matthew 18:27). The king cancelled the debt. Compassion led him to understand that the man was not the issue. The real issue was what he was losing and his anger at that loss if this man did not repay him. I had been doing this forgiveness thing all wrong!

Prison time for the offender would not address the king's loss. Even if the man were being tortured, the king had still lost a considerable amount of money and even reputation, and torture could never replace it or give back to him what had been taken. Initially, he was determined to have justice and vengeance by throwing the man into prison. But what did that achieve? What does vengeance (which we often disguise as justice) actually achieve? The king would still have lost his money, and everyone would be afraid of him, walking on eggshells, cautious in their dealings with him in case they also fell victim to his anger and sense of (in) justice. I think many people felt like that around me. I know for a long time my wife did. She never knew what might set me off and cause me to rail at her for some stupid or imagined slight.

Often in my attempts at forgiveness I wrestled with the

person I was offended by. My focus was on *them*, what *they* did to me and how I would like to repay them. Rather than alleviating pain and loss, it fed something more primal within and kept the reservoir of hate and anger topped up. I had built up a great sense of injustice in my heart, keeping a record of the many offences against me, and had stored up so many grudges and resentments over the years that I could no longer keep count of them individually. I learned how to keep grudges and never forget what others had done to me. I judged people harshly. One offence was enough to put you in my bad books.

The king's anger, his desire for justice was not about the man's behaviour; it was about his own sense of injustice or unfairness at his loss. Perhaps he felt foolish for allowing it to go on so long, and this made him angry too. Many things have happened to make me feel foolish and fueled my anger.

These days, I have arrived at the place where I no longer think the person offending me is the issue to be dealt with. Forgiveness, as it has traditionally been taught, focuses on the person and releasing them from your anger and resentment, but it robs us of true freedom as we keep wrestling. I am now coming to see it from a different perspective. Forgiveness means to let go of or to give up and carries the idea of separation from something[9]. I tried, on numerous

---

9. The Greek word Aphiemi, is the word Jesus uses in Matthew 18. For further explanation see www.preceptaustin.org/forgive-aphiemi-greek-word-study

occasions, letting go of the person and giving up my anger against them.

I understand now that the person was never the issue. The real issue was my pain, the wound I carried. It was never really about what someone had done to me. The events were never the real issue. My loss and the attitude of my heart to it was the real issue.

The king in Matthew's story changed. Initially, it was all about being paid back, restitution being made, and justice enacted in a display of power. But instead of dealing with the person and taking his anger, frustration and resentment out on the person, the king dealt with the issue that lay between them. The real issue wasn't what the servant had done. It was what the king had lost and was trying to claw back.

The issue for me was not what the person did, but what I was hanging on to – the idea of revenge. In order to be free from his loss, the king needed to let go of the debt, separate himself from it and give up any thought of it being restored to him. The king gave up the loss and cancelled the entire debt, erasing any record of it. When the debt was cancelled, there was no longer an issue between them and no reason to hold anything against the person.

When I began to address my pain, I changed my focus and dealt with the real issue. In our focus on the person, we wrestle with letting them go and trying to do something which our hearts often do not feel or even want, and it focuses us away from the real issue of pain, offence and wounding.

In Ephesians 6:12, the apostle Paul tells us that our struggle is not with flesh and blood. People are not the issue to be faced down and grappled into submission or manipulated into defeat. In 2 Corinthians 10:4, he warns us that our weapons are not the weapons of this world. The aggression, violence and confrontational tactics of our cultures are not the ways in which believers are to face challenges. Our weapons are love, forgiveness, kindness and gentleness not getting even.

As we turn our focus away from the person and look at why we are offended and where the pain is, then, we bring that before Father, allowing his love to change and soften our hearts. As he brings healing, we can let go of the offence and pain and there is no longer anything between us and that person. It doesn't happen overnight, but the more we live in love the easier it becomes to let go of real issues.

I reconciled myself to the reality that I had lost something, and that person was never going to be able to give it back to me. He didn't have the ability to do that. As I accepted that reality, I found that I began to let go of my pain and anger. For a long time, I have said that, although I no longer want to harm that man, I have not reached a place of compassion for him. I have no desire to be in his vicinity or in his company. However, I recently heard he had suffered a misfortune, and I actually felt a little bit sorry for him, for the way it happened.

The emotion took me completely by surprise. I did not expect to feel anything for him, but heart forgiveness really works! I have not seen him since that happened those years ago, but I am expecting that if / when I do, my reaction will not be what it would have been. Perhaps I may even be able to have a conversation, who knows?

One of the other 'benefits' I've noticed in this whole process is that the deeper I go into love and learn not to 'wrestle with flesh and blood", the less quickly I take offence. I was at a meeting some time ago where I bumped into an acquaintance. We stopped and chatted for a few minutes before he had to rush off, but the friend I was with was rather annoyed. When I asked him what was wrong, he was quite adamant that my acquaintance had been rude to me. I had no idea what he was talking about and still do not.

As heart forgiveness and living in love becomes a lifestyle for us, offence finds it difficult to gain a hold upon our hearts. The freedom this brings is incredible.

In another example I want to mention a break in at our home. I had just returned from teaching a Father-heart Ministries A School in England and had some of the finances from it in my possession. During the night of my return, someone got into the house and stole computer equipment, some other personal items and almost 2,000 British Pounds (GBP).

I didn't forgive the person who did it because, incredibly, I felt no animosity towards them. I was upset about the losses of course and disappointed, but I 'took that on the chin' and didn't feel any desire for revenge or payback. I was in a place where I trusted Father to look out for us, and he did. In fact, some of the items were recovered by the police, although nine months passed before I could retake possession of them. Due to the legal process, I was more annoyed with the police than the robber!

I wish every single time someone did something I could react in those ways, but the truth is I'm a child in the ways of love and forgiveness and I'm still growing in it. I look for the day when offence, no matter how great, will not affect me. In the meantime, I am learning to enjoy the journey of being loved back to life.

The way of our Father is not through forced behaviour or repetitive prayers. That is how religion operates. Father's way is not by a system or a programme, but through a changed heart. There is an old saying where I come from, *"To err is human and to forgive is divine."* I think there is a truth in that. There can often be nothing within the human heart that desires to forgive. What we really want is revenge, a feeling that we are owed something. While that feeling persists, our hearts are not truly free. We are still captive to offence, like the servant in Jesus' story.

If true forgiveness is from the heart and that heart has nothing in it that wants to forgive, then that heart needs to change, and only divine love is capable of changing our hearts. There are no systems or programmes created by man that have that kind of capability, no matter how anointed the creator of such programmes may be.

Letting go is a process. It is not an instant, magic potion or formula. Working through loss and pain can take considerable time. The process I described above has taken me close to five years from beginning to end. Expect this journey to take time as we continue to pour our hearts out to him. I no longer look to God to change other people; I expect him to change **my** heart.

Over the years, since the encounter I described in the first chapter, love has slowly but surely been changing me from a bitter, judgmental individual with a grudge against the world into someone completely different. I'm beginning to understand love and its power. I'm starting to grasp how important it is in the future of this world. As I've seen what love has begun in me and is continuing to do, I am more than ever convinced that love is the answer to ALL of the world's problems. It isn't an easy, sentimental answer which makes us feel warm and fuzzy.

As we learn to allow love to penetrate our hearts the transformation is far beyond the ability of all the religious systems, ministry prayers and inner healing programmes we could ever come up with.

CHAPTER 13

MY PERSPECTIVE
OF LOVE

"Love is the answer" sings Soul/R&B artist Aloe Blacc [10] and The Beatles told us *"Love is All You Need."* [11]

Love is the focus of movies, music, art and novels yet there seems to be a distinct lack of love in our cultures and societies. We say things like, *"I love my wife"*, *"I love choco-late"*, *"I love movies"*, *"I love soccer"* and they are all uttered with equal passion so that it can be difficult to determine which has priority when hearing the words or seeing them written. The reality of love is way beyond our shallow under-standing of it as a mere romantic or sexual expression of desire and passion.

The apostle Paul writes about the nature of love and we use it for weddings because we equate love with romance,

---

10. Love is the Answer, track 4 from the studio album, *Lift Your Spirit*, (Interscope Records) released October 25, 2013

11. 7-inch vinyl single released 7 July 1967, (Parlaphone Records)

but let's take a look at the scriptures and see what Paul is saying.

He exposes the Corinthians' gatherings as rabbles and their relationships as severely dysfunctional. Their use of spiritual gifts was highlighting their divisions, jealousies and

unwholesome behaviour so Paul decides to tackle it more subtly. Rather than issuing a whole series of rebukes, he appeals to their ego and selfish ambitions. In 1 Corinthians 12:31, he teases them by saying, *"eagerly desire the greater gifts."* Now he has their attention! Then he continues in the same vein, *"And now I will show you the most excellent way."*

1 Corinthians 13:1-3 *"If I speak in the tongues of men and*

of angels, but have not love, I am only a resounding gong or a clanging cymbal. If I have the gift of prophecy and can fathom all mysteries and all knowledge, and if I have a faith that can move mountains, but have not love, I am nothing. If I give all I possess to the poor and surrender my body to the flames, but have not love, I gain nothing".

He addresses the performance and ambition of Christians not only in first century Corinth but everywhere. The gifts he mentions are prominent and easily seen, drawing attention to the user and elevating their profile. We see the same today, a desire for prominence and recognition in ministry.

Paul draws them in by inferring he has some esoteric knowledge that has escaped the Corinthian Church, *"now I will show you the most excellent way."* It is an old trick still in use today. It's why so many confidence-tricks work both secular and spiritual. He starts off with the gifts they have been so eager to display (*the tongues of men and of angels, prophecy and fathom all mysteries*) and their super spiritual behaviour (*faith that can move mountains; give all to the poor*) by telling them that these things alone are insufficient for true spirituality.

He is bringing them a new perspective of Christian living.

I have read these scriptures so many times and preached on them in church, but I have been theologically conditioned over the years to the point that I missed what Paul is saying. Too often, I have read the scriptures without realising what they actually say. I have read something and thought, "*I have to do this*" or "*I already have this.*"

We have been trained to believe that the effectiveness of our Christianity is measured by what we do. Often when we read scripture, we come with this question, "*What must I do to be the Christian God wants me to be?*" When reading this particular passage, the default is to ask how to '*do*' love, create strategies for being a loving person or programmes to enable people to *do* loving things. We pay for strangers' coffee or dinner, pay their bridge tolls because this is '*doing*' love. Somehow, we have convinced ourselves that this evangelistic strategy is fulfilling the instruction to love others.

We strive to be 'nice' to others and look out for others' needs but Paul is not telling us that we can have spiritual gifts as long as we "*do*" love; he states that we can have all the gifts but if we do not <u>have</u> love, then it is pointless. Love is not about our actions; it is all about our hearts. Do our hearts contain love or is some other force motivating us?

1 Corinthians 13:4-8a tells us, "*Love is patient, love is kind. It does not envy, it does not boast, it is not proud. It is not rude, it is not self- seeking, it is not easily angered, it keeps no record of wrongs. Love does not delight in evil but rejoices with the truth. It always protects, always trusts, always hopes,*

always perseveres. Love never fails."

I had always thought that Paul is speaking about human behaviour in this passage and I had to learn to cultivate loving behaviour in order to prove myself. I perceived that it was like a recipe book of how to make a Christian and how to produce Christian living. I would put my effort, my will toward fulfilling this prescription because this is what a Christian looks like.

BUT Paul is not saying, *"this is what you have to do."* He is saying, *"This is what it looks like when love has found a dwelling within you. This is what love will produce in your heart."* He is speaking about internal motivation of the heart, and he is telling us that if there is not love in our hearts, if our heart is not in the place where it experiences love constantly being received, then all of our efforts to produce the fruit of love, is **nothing**; all of the great things we do mean **nothing** and the sacrifices and miracles are worthless in kingdom value.

We chase supernatural ministry and manifestations believing that this is how the world will be changed and won, how we will demonstrate the greatness of God (and these things do have their place; I love healing and prophecy). But the fact is that unless love is the motivating factor then God takes little notice of what we are doing.

"The Lord does not look at the things man looks at. Man

looks at the outward appearance, but the Lord looks at the heart." (1Samuel16:7)

Paul is echoing that statement when he writes to the Corinthians regarding their behaviour and the most excellent way of love. He is telling us that love will put these things into our heart. It is not our job to try and replicate loving deeds but to receive love and allow that love to transform us from the inside. When we do that, love will create a patient heart, a kind heart and these behaviours will not be learned but will spring forth from the overflow.

Jesus told us on many occasions that what is in our hearts is what will manifest most (Luke 6:45; Mark 7:21-22), especially in unguarded moments. We can, like the Corinthians, attempt to do loving things in the absence of indwelling love, but it will only be empty gesturing and posturing like *'a resounding gong or a clanging cymbal'*. So often our identity is rooted in what we do and how well we do it as though our performance determines worth.

Paul comes against this belief by telling the church that you can do wonderful things, spiritual and nice things but if love is not dwelling within, then you have nothing, you are nothing and all you do means nothing. That is quite hard hitting for our results driven faith communities and activists. Paul tells his readers that unless they have love, their spiritual activities are worthless and then goes on in verse four to describe love.

What he is communicating is that love will produce these things within us; love will make us patient and kind, lacking envy and pride and quick to forgive. Kindness will become an automatic behaviour; selfishness will lose its grip on you and anger will no longer control you. Scripture is talking about a disposition of the heart that is brought about by love being received (1John 4:19). Will power or following programmes and strategies do not produce this kind of life!

When the Bible says love is kind, it is speaking about a person who lives out of the kindness they have experienced and received in their heart. Unless you experience kindness, you cannot know what it is like and cannot effectively convey it to others. You may mimic the actions of a kind person but that doesn't make you kind. **It merely makes you a good mimic.**

So much of what we are taught in Christianity today is a parody of reality and we have become good mimics. Jesus did not do all He did via a programme and neither did He have a strategy. He lived so deeply in His Father's love that He could say, *"I tell you the truth, the Son can do nothing by himself; he can do only what he sees his Father doing, because whatever the Father does the Son also does. For the Father loves the Son and shows him all he does..."*

When love touches our hearts, it changes our perspective

and we see differently. When we see things from a different perspective it will affect our behaviour much more deeply than studying the Bible to learn new ways to behave. There is a desperation in people to be noticed and recognised that can lead to performance spirituality. But Paul is telling us, *"Let Love dwell in you and if Love dwells in you, Love will produce these characteristics in you and you will be patient, kind, etc."*

Until recent years, I had always lived with episodes of having touches from God and then thinking that was me charged up to fight the battle again (but which has, in reality, already been won). What God really wants to do is pour the substance of His Love into our hearts, into the depths of our being because that's where the need is.

When we know what it is to be loved in that way, deep within our beings, and Love dwells and permeates our whole being THEN we begin to see the fruit of Love growing in our lives effortlessly (Galatians 5:22). I am no longer interested in getting touches from God. I want to learn to live in a place where Love dwells in me and I 'have' Love.

This passage of scripture in first Corinthians, describes how Father relates to and treats his children, how He approaches the ones He loves. Love is a statement of who God is, a manifestation of The Divine essence. That's why John says that God is love, and as we read 1 Corinthians

13 replacing the word love with Father, perhaps we begin to understand that God our Father is not standing at a distance sending something to us, disinterestedly, but is actually imparting something of Himself to dwell within our being.

For some reason, we have not understood that God the Father is patient with us (2 Peter 3:9). Instead we have painted the portrait of a deity with a hair trigger temperament who must be feared and appeased.

But the list of Love's qualities by Paul reveals the true nature and character of God as a Father to us.

- *Father is patient*
- *Father is kind*
- *Father does not envy*
- *He does not boast*
- *He is not proud*
- *Father is not rude*
- *He is not self-seeking*
- *Nor is He easily angered*
- *Father keeps no record of wrongs*
- *Father does not delight in evil*
- *Father rejoices in the truth*

- *Father always protects*
- *Father always trusts*
- *Father always hopes*
- *Father always perseveres*
- *Father never fails*

As he pours his Love into our hearts, we will learn to keep no records of other people's wrongs AND none of our own wrongs. Often the list we keep, of our faults, is so long we develop a sense of failure in living the Christian life but the truth is that *God was reconciling the world to himself in Christ, not counting men's sins against them* (2Cor.5:19).

Love is the most powerful transforming force I know of, and His love poured into our hearts will transform us from the inside out. As Paul tells us in 2 Corinthians 3:18 *"we all with unveiled face, beholding the glory of the Lord, are being transformed into his image from one degree of glory to another"*.

When Adam was fashioned from the dust of the earth, God came close and breathed into his nostrils. Something from within the being of God was placed inside the man causing him to live as an image of his Father. An impartation of the essence of God Himself birthed a son in His own image and that is exactly what He is doing today in this revelation. He is rebirthing and restoring sons and daughters. God is imparting something of His own essence into the hearts of human beings (Romans 5:5) and it is bringing us more and more back to the Garden where we understand ourselves as made in His image.

LOVE'S COVERING

A while ago, I met someone for the first time and they told me a mutual friend had said, *"You'll like John. He's a bit strange, but you'll like him."* I prefer to think of myself as unique and I was much more of a unique individual in my young days.

I used to go to the Saturday morning movies as a kid. I remember going to the cinema one Saturday morning wearing yellow trousers with black stripes. The other kids laughed, and I thought, *"They don't have a clue."* I liked being different and standing out even in those preteen years. Over time, I found that other people made fun of the things I liked or said, how I dressed, etc. They laughed at my clothes and the way I spoke.

It became too much for me as I grew up, and I eventually began to believe that being me was not a good thing. I began to reinvent who John MacDonald was.

No one likes being different or standing out too much. Being ridiculed for being yourself is not an enjoyable or desirable experience. I felt as though I did not fit and being made fun of or excluded for being me confirmed all the ungodly beliefs, I had about myself, about my worth and my value as an individual (I was not wanted, everything was my fault). I began to learn how to fit in, and I began to like the same things other people liked to fit in. That worked really well when I became a Christian.

I have realised that much of what we do in life is in an attempt to fit in, to be one of the crowd, and be accepted. Peer pressure is an incredibly powerful force in a person's life. Many people who say they don't want to be conventional have adopted the position of exiles, because, wanting to fit in but unable to do so, they need to find some way to avoid the pain and suffering that comes from not being with the 'in crowd'.

The problem this creates is that we begin to live our lives as someone else and not the person we were created to be. That's what I was doing for many years. I was living the life of someone else who looked like John MacDonald. I was trying to blend in rather than stand out (like Adam hiding in the trees), looking to others to validate me and give my existence some kind of worth.

We can go through life with a feeling of being 'not right', not good enough, the sense that there is something wrong with being me. It is like an itch that cannot be scratched. No matter what you do, you cannot get comfortable. We spend our lives looking for something that will make us good enough, that will allow us to fit in.

The idea of being vulnerable and 'found out' drives us to hide the real me; but covering up and hiding who we are doesn't work. The fear of being found out doesn't allow us to live a restful, at ease life and we never become comfortable. When we are willing to be vulnerable and say, "*Here I am.*"; when we are willing to let people see us, then we can begin to lose that sense of discomfort, that nagging feeling of being 'not right'.

Why was I living life being someone I was not?

Why was I unable to be who I am?

I believe this goes back to the garden. In Genesis 3:6, we read, "*When the woman saw that the fruit of the tree was good for food and pleasing to the eye, and also desirable for gaining wisdom, she took some and ate it. She also gave some to her husband, who was with her, and he ate it. Then the eyes of both of them were opened, and they realised they were naked; so, they sewed fig leaves together and made coverings for themselves."*

At the fall, Adam and his wife came into an experience that they had never been through before. They felt vulnerable and uncovered. The sense of intimacy and relationship with Father felt broken. The union of hearts was broken and as they looked at themselves and each other, they attempted to cover it up.

The physical nakedness revealed their soul's nakedness and as something changed within their hearts, they became uncomfortable being themselves and tried to cover up who they really were in an attempt to blend in with their surroundings and hide even from each other. Covering up helped them feel better about themselves and they could hide their awkwardness and vulnerability. This desire and attempt of ours at fitting in is a continuation of those first human's attempts at covering their nakedness, an attempt to pretend that nothing is wrong in order to appear presentable and acceptable.

The terrible lie we believe is that being me is not enough, so we cover up, presenting to others the person we think they want to see. We are afraid to be seen by others for who we really are. I think we are often afraid to be seen by God for who we really are and so we present to Him the person we think He wants us to be.

Religion is built on the fear of not being enough. That is

the basis of our religious systems and what drives religious behaviour. So, we have unwritten lists of the things that are necessary to be 'good' Christians. We have the pressure to follow the 'prescription'.

- *Memorise scripture*
- *Keep the quiet time*
- *Witness at every opportunity*
- *Pray fervently*
- *Keep the rules*
- *Attend the meetings*
- *Fast*
- *Be obedient*
- *Read the scriptures diligently*
- *Have right doctrine and theology*

Once we have made ourselves presentable, then we are ready to face the world. Often worried that we might say or do the wrong thing and no longer fit in. While we fit in, we can exude an air of, *"Look at me, I have it together."*

When we are alone, when it is only me and God, then there is no one left to fool, and we are left with the real me. Many people cannot cope with the real them. They cannot cope with the pressure of trying to be what is acceptable to the world – wearing the things, the attitudes, the clothes. Suddenly, they cannot hide from themselves and a person fails or commits suicide because the pressure of pretending, the pain of the struggle, becomes too much and is so powerful that they only see one way out.

Since the fall, the human condition has been such that we feel driven and strive to cover up the real me – to put up a façade that will deflect attention away from the real me.

WHAT CAN BE DONE?

When Adam and his wife saw their nakedness, when they felt the shift within their souls, they felt the need to cover up and sewed fig leaves together before they could present themselves to Father. We still feel the need to do that.

They misunderstood His love and affection for them, thinking He would no longer find them acceptable and we still live in that misunderstanding; thinking that He doesn't find us acceptable any longer because of what we are, because of what we have done or not done, because we are not good enough Christians.

When we sin, it causes us to feel conviction, and the accompanying sense of guilt can cause us to hide from Father rather than come to Him; just like those first humans in the garden, after eating from the tree of The Knowledge of Good and Evil. Even in putting them out of the garden Father was loving His kids not turning from them or punishing them. He also demonstrated his love in another way.

Genesis 3:21 *The LORD* God made garments of skin for Adam and his wife and clothed them. In his love, He reclothed the man and his wife without them having 'repented'. Before they had to leave the garden and face whatever, whoever was out there, God himself made them acceptable out of the provision of his love, despite their refusal to accept responsibility for what happened. We have put such emphasis on the need for repentance, yet God does not ask for this from Adam and his wife before ministering to them.

Love covers our broken humanity.

His love covered Adam and his wife in the brokenness of their humanity, and He does the same for us. If we are willing to allow ourselves to be seen, if we will take the courage to become the real vulnerable me, He covers us in love.

Vulnerability feels scary to me because I have lived so long with my own coverings rather than His love covering me. I am on a journey of learning to divest myself of my own coverings which at times leaves me feeling really exposed and naked. BUT the more I open to His love, the more I know His love covering me the more I can be vulnerable and the covering of His love enables me to live life as John rather than living life as the person you think is John.

I read a quote from Brene Brown which really spoke to me: *"Let go of who you think you're supposed to be and embrace who you are."*[12]

We have created identities for ourselves so that we fit in. My big covering was being cool, unaffected by life, not getting excited or upset or emotional by circumstances or events.

True confidence comes from the covering of his love that goes beyond anything else. It is more than the covering of religious behaviour that makes us look good and acceptable; that is just another false covering to make us feel like we fit in. When we know Father's love for us, there is a confidence that allows us to stand tall before ANYONE – authorities, the wealthy or the powerful – without any sense of lack or inferiority and without feeling like we need to blend in.

It is time to come out from the bushes and allow him to re-clothe you with his love.

---

12. *The Gifts of Imperfection.* Center City, MN: Hazelden (2010)

A HEART AT REST

I am convinced that unless we come to know God as our Father, we will not experience intimacy with Him. My ambition as a believer was to be a servant of God. But as I have journeyed in this revelation of Love, I have discovered another way of living.

Servants do not have intimacy with the Father of the house – only sons have that intimacy. That's what the the writer of Hebrews is speaking about in chapter one, when they compare God's relationship with Jesus the Son, to His relationship with angels, who are servants (Heb.1:14). Servants can have experiences and encounters, and that's the language I hear in Christendom today - the need for encounters with the power of God. Great, go for it. BUT these encounters will not satisfy; they will not give you comfort, satisfaction or rest unless there is intimacy as that between son and Father.

Intimacy is not about irregular encounters as servants. Sons **LIVE** in the place of intimacy - they do not just visit there. This intimacy is the result of ongoing personal inter-action between people in relationship and it doesn't matter where you are or what you are doing in the world, you are constantly aware of closeness and an unbroken connection.

My relationship with my wife is the result of years of personal interaction between us, and it has produced an intimacy and created a bond and connection between us that is difficult to disrupt. It doesn't matter where I am in the world, I am aware of my wife. I am aware of my connection to her and her to me. It is the same in our relationship with Father. For too many years, my 'relationship' with God consisted of Bible reading, attending meetings, keeping the rules and obeying his commands.

It is only in the last few years, after twenty plus years as a believer, that I have begun to actually enter into *real* relationship with God. Don't get me wrong, I was born again, Spirit-filled and could hear the voice of God. Any servant can do that. We throw around cute religious phrases like, *"it isn't a religion, it's a relationship,"* but the truth is that millions of Christians around the world do not experience relationship. We follow a code, keep to the prescription of what a Christian should be, should do, should say BUT do not have that constant awareness of intimate relationship and connection with Father.

Praying and reading the Bible does not equate to intimacy. Neither does serving in ministry.

On this journey, I am learning to come as a little child, trusting completely that Father is good and has only my best interests at the heart of all He does and all He says. Like a little child, I am learning to let go of striving, of trying harder to be a better Christian and it is bringing me into rest and a place of intimacy and vulnerability. I'm not all the way in living a life of complete transparency and openness but I am much nearer to it than I have ever been.

I want to say something about rest. I am becoming more and more convinced that this is one of the foundations of our sonship. **Jesus lived in rest**. That is why he could say in Matthew 11:28, *"Come to me, all you who are weary and burdened, and I will give you rest."* Jesus is not speaking to people who have been working hard and are now exhausted.

It isn't for those physically tired but those who are weighed down with cares and worries, who are burdened by the things which weigh us down, slow us up, or cause us to give up.

Jesus knew what it was to live in rest and live out of a place of rest, so he could 'give' it to us. He can introduce us to a lifestyle of rest.

Jesus, the Last Adam (1 Corinthians 15:45), came to recover all that the first Adam lost; one of which was rest. Adam's first day as a conscious being was God's Sabbath day, God's day of rest. When God finished breathing into Adam's nostrils, he finished his 'work'. Adam didn't see that work, so all he knew from his first waking moment was rest. His introduction to life on earth was to enter God's rest.

Children imitate their parents; whether we like it or not, they will, and I believe Adam was no different. He would imitate God and so God rested on Adam's first day, and what Adam learned and copied from his Father was how to live life out of a place of rest. He had no pressure to copy God's creative acts or displays of power. He only had to rest in Father's love, presence, provision and intimacy.

We know Adam worked at a later date. God told him to subdue the earth, but he was in a place of inner rest constantly. I wonder what work looks like when carried out from such a place of rest. Adam wasn't driven; he didn't have to prove to Father he was capable and competent. He didn't have to compete with his wife to be the best worker, and he wasn't under pressure to produce; there were no targets set by God, for him to meet.

I believe that much of our own absence of rest comes down to the question of whether we trust God or not. Rest doesn't come from the absence of activity; it comes from the absence of worry and drivenness. For Adam, what was there to worry about; there was no driving force pushing him on to perform and achieve. His Father had provided life, a place to live, food, companionship. There was no ambition or strife. Father's love taught Adam to trust and it is this trust that enables us to rest.

In modern Christendom, we can be anxious that we don't do enough, pray enough, witness enough and our Christianity is lived out against a background of fear, of not measuring up, of not doing enough. Adam trusted that, even in physical rest and inactivity, Father was loving him and providing for him and when Adam walked out of the garden, in his heart, he was walking out of trust and rest. Worry and strife became a normal part of human experience.

Jesus addressed this anxiety in Matthew 6:25-33 when he tells us not to worry because Father will provide. When we learn to trust His provision, to trust that He knows what He is doing with our lives then we can rest and begin to let go of the worry and fear.

Where is this rest from? Where did Jesus rest come from? Psalms 62:1 *My soul finds rest in God alone; my salvation comes from him.* David tells us that only God can give us rest. In Psalms 131:2, he tells us what that looks like, "*like a weaned child with its mother, like a weaned child is my soul within me*".

We look to so many things to ease the discomfort of our souls – work, reputation, wealth, addictions, but it is only at the bosom of the Father we can find that ease and comfort. The reason Jesus was at rest, even in the midst of a busy schedule or at sea in a storm, was because He knows the Father and is known by Him.

Jesus rests in the place of intimacy against Father's breast. "*No one has ever seen God, but God the One and Only, who is at the Father's side, has made him known.*" John 1:18.[13]

From the place at his Father's bosom, Jesus walks intimately with Abba and knows Himself being loved and fathered. Jesus has prepared a place there for *us* at Father's bosom so that we may know the same level of intimacy and come to the same level of trust and rest.

"*Do not let your hearts be troubled. "Do not let your hearts*

---

13. The word translated side by the NIV is 'kolpos' which means the space between the arms, thus the bosom.

be troubled. Trust in God; trust also in me. In my Father's house are many rooms; if it were not so, I would have told you. I am going there to prepare a place for you. And if I go and prepare a place for you, I will come back and take you to be with me that you also may be where I am. (John 14:1-3).

When others are burning out, you can know heart rest, your strength being renewed.

As we read scripture, we see that Jesus was often busy and even when He seeks physical rest, He ends up ministering. What then is this rest He speaks of? The following scriptures mainly speak about the physical realm in which we live, but they provide a picture of what Father intends for our hearts. We can see a picture in them of what He intends for us as we come to that place of intimacy on His bosom.

Job 3:25-26 *"What I feared has come upon me; what I dreaded has happened to me. I have no peace, no quietness; I have no rest, but only turmoil."*

Rest is the absence of turmoil which is the result of fear and worry (v.25), the things which rob us of peace. Job was in the midst of great turmoil which robbed him of trust and forced him into an environment of worry and fearful antic-ipation which caused him to lose sight of God's goodness.

We often quote the Bible, *"There is no fear in love. But perfect love drives out fear,"* (1 John 4:18). When scripture speaks of perfect love casting out fear, it is not referring to a theology or doctrine. It is speaking of the experience of being loved so deeply in an ongoing impartation from the bosom of Father that fear begins to be uprooted in the love experience.

It is learning to live at Father's breast and as we receive and trust His love for us. The peace and rest love brings to our hearts causes fear, worry and anxiety to lose their hold and cease to be the driving, motivating factors in our lives. Jesus in rest means He is in a place where Father is releasing His heart from fear, worry and anxiety, from conflict of heart and uncertainty about Himself.

True heart rest is the absence of worry and anxiety, the absence of insecurity and conflict and uncertainty about ourselves, like a child at its mother's breast. At a mother's breast is where a baby learns to trust, so Father invites us, in Christ, to **His** breast to learn afresh what it is to be loved and to trust in the provision of that love. It is out of that place of trust that we gain the ability to rest.

1 Chronicles 22:9 *But you will have a son who will be a man of peace and rest, and I will give him rest from all his enemies on every side. His name will be Solomon, and I will grant Israel peace and quiet during his reign.*

2 Chronicles 20:30 *"...the kingdom of Jehoshaphat was at peace, for his God had given him rest on every side."*

The absence of conflict is a mark of rest. We can experience an absence of internal conflict about who we are and who our Father is, free from conflict over his love and provision for us. He will not let us down. This inner peace will also result in a lack of conflict with others because we will not feel the need to assert ourselves and our 'rights' or to raise ourselves up and win arguments with others.

Isaiah 14:7 *"All the lands are at rest and at peace; they break into singing."*

Joy and peace are marks of a heart at rest. It seems as though I have been in so many Christian meetings where we are being told that we need to be more joyful and are encouraged in the singing to be full of joy.

There is such a paucity of understanding and experience of joy that it seems as though it needs to be worked up from our own meagre, emotional resources. Congregations are whipped up by worship leaders and pastors to enthusiastically express 'the joy of the Lord'.

Joy can never be created by external things or by self-effort; it is the result of an inner attitude and position of our hearts and the peace that comes can be a strange sensation and experience, but as we learn to live in it, peace becomes a familiar state of being for us and joy is a constant in our lives. We will not have to work it up at all.

Why is rest so important? Why do we speak of it so much? Rest is what you were made to live from. I wrote earlier about Adam being birthed into rest and everything he did coming out of that starting position of rest. Rest is an attitude and position that comes from recognising something has been accomplished.

This rest I am speaking about is something arising from a recognition that all things that are necessary are already accomplished and there is no need to stress and strive about them.

We simply watch it unfold.

This rest brings us to a place of peace and release from worry and anxiety; we can experience freedom from the inner conflicts in our heart, the turmoil that causes us to live driven lives as we seek to prove ourselves and prove to others that we are worth something, that our lives matter.

The soul conflicts that cause us to be performers and attention seekers, ill at ease and uncomfortable in our own skin are no longer driving forces in our lives when we understand that ALL things have been decided already, from before the foundations of the earth (Math.25:34; Eph.1:4).

Hebrews 4:9-10 *"There remains, then, a Sabbath-rest for the people of God; for anyone who enters God's rest also rests from his own work, just as God did from his."*

This rest frees us from the need to strive and perform. Like Adam, our hearts can enter Father's Sabbath rest. He was not conflicted over his Father's affection for him and when we are in a place of trusting Father, we can rest in the certainty that He has our best interests in mind, and we do not need to look after our own best interests. This frees us up to look out for the interests of others (Philippians 2:3,4).

Before Jesus returned to this place of trust on the Father's bosom, he said, *"I'm making a place for you at the Father's bosom too so that where I am you will be also."* Father's Love is the key. It is Father who gives us rest as we come to him (Psalm 62) and receive his love being poured into our hearts.

I often wondered why I struggled so much with the ability to rest, and it was only recently when I was teaching on Father's mothering heart that I began to understand. The scripture says that Jesus and the Father will make their home in us; that we become a place where love can dwell rather than visit (John 14:23).

For many, love is a visitor rather than a resident. We were designed to receive and contain that love, nurture, sense of safety and peace at our mothers' breast. In a fallen state that often does not happen, but in the new birth Father decided that we should be brought to His breast to receive the love that we need, to be nurtured and learn trust there.

This is a process. It doesn't happen overnight, but as we

learn to remain at His bosom allowing His love to nurture our spirits and feed our souls, like Adam and Jesus, we will know freedom from fear, anxiety and worry. We will know peace and joy in the rest that Father alone gives. That's what the cross made possible.

We are not just forgiven, not just placed into sonship, not just cleansed but brought to the bosom of the Father Himself who loves you. It is an ongoing, continual process and a fantastic journey that brings us deeper into the place of inner rest free from conflict, turmoil, fear and worry into a peaceful, joy filled life. That has been my increasing experience over the years since I consciously encountered Father. It is the increasing experience of many people around the world too.

I am discovering what it means to be His son and live in love.

My whole understanding of God, life and Christianity has been, and continues to be, turned upside down and yet I am finding life becoming more peaceful, less stressful and infinitely more enjoyable. I have no time for regrets of the past any longer because the present is so much better than I ever imagined it could be and the future is already taken care of because we have a great big Dad who loves us and intends only good for our lives.

Lake Como, Italy 2014

If you'd like to stay up to date with John MacDonald's latest publications, please visit his website:

www.sonship.co.uk

Lightning Source UK Ltd.
Milton Keynes UK
UKHW020616311019
352616UK00010B/650/P